Inheriting an IRA

Professional Edition

INHERITING
AN IRA

PROFESSIONAL EDITION

MICHAEL J. JONES

This publication is designed to provide accurate and authoritative information in regard to the subject matter covered. It is sold with the understanding that the publisher and the author are not engaged in rendering legal, accounting or other professional services. If legal advice or other professional assistance is required, the services of a competent professional should be sought.

Published by Paddleboard Press, LLC
24591 Silver Cloud Court, Suite 250, Monterey, CA 93940. 831.373.1800

Cover design: Michael McDaniel

ISBN-10: 0-9914104-1-6
ISBN-13: 978-0-9914104-1-5

*In memory of Jerry A. Kasner, dear
friend and mentor to many*

Contents

PART 1
THE INHERITED IRA OPPORTUNITY

PART 2
INHERITED IRA-SPEAK

PART 3
REQUIRED MINIMUM DISTRIBUTIONS –
YOU INHERITED AN IRA FROM THE IRA'S CREATOR

PART 4
REQUIRED MINIMUM DISTRIBUTIONS -
YOU INHERITED AN INHERITED IRA

PART 5
GOING DEEPER

ACKNOWLEDGEMENTS

IN 2012, DIANA NYAD fulfilled at age 64 her lifetime dream of competing a solo open ocean swim from Cuba to Florida. This she did after five attempts, starting at age 35. Upon reaching shore, she said:

> I have three messages. One is we should never ever give
> up. Two is you never are too old to chase your dreams.
> Three is it looks like a solitary sport but it takes a team.

Likewise, when it comes to producing a book, authorship looks like a solitary "sport" but it takes a team.

Dawn Markowitz cheerfully provided copy editing by kind permission of Trusts & Estates magazine. Natalie Choate, author of *Life And Death Planning For Retirement Plans* (www.ataxplan.com), also provided editing and technical review, as did Michael Miller. DeeAnn Thompson, my dear spouse and business partner, more or less lived with this project, providing editing, helpful questioning, debate, design and formatting. Michael McDaniel created the book's cover and some additional graphics with startling creativity and speed.

Not only can a book not be produced alone, but also Inherited IRA rules can't be comprehended without the perspectives of other professionals. In my case, these include: the late Professor Jerry A. Kasner, Natalie B. Choate, Steven E. Trytten, Ed Slott, Stephen J. Krass, Robert S. Keebler, Barry C. Picker, Michelle L. Ward, Bruce D. Steiner, Guerdon Ely, Beverly DeVeny, Denise Appleby, Professor Christopher R. Hoyt, Seymour Goldberg, Alvin J. Golden, Jeffrey Levine and Jane Schuck.

INTRODUCTION

Even for very smart professionals, it's not hard to make costly mistakes—so arm yourself with information and ask lots of questions, before you decide what to do

IT'S MY HOPE THAT this book will help you in your quest to make the most out of your inherited Individual Retirement Account or "IRA". Over its chapters, you'll be able to glean critical information about IRAs that you, as a beneficiary, have complete control over, meaning, you have the right to withdraw as much as you want from your Inherited IRA and also have the right to direct how the IRA is invested. This book is also useful if you inherited any other kind of retirement account and can make a direct transfer to an Inherited IRA.

I'm going to show you how taking out the least annual amount required by our tax laws will make your Inherited IRA deliver the most value to you over your lifetime. But it's ultimately up to you to decide if you have some other reason for taking out more than you must.

I was inspired to write this work by everyday questions I address about Inherited IRAs. Those questions come from IRA inheritors as well as from my professional friends in the fields of accounting, law, investment management, and philanthropy. I wrote it for IRA inheritors and their advisors to use together because I have found that an informed IRA inheritor working together with a knowledgeable advisor consistently produces the best results.

You won't have to become an expert in order to handle your Inherited IRA the right way. Over three decades of practice, I have found that, as with so many "complex" things, about 20 percent of what's in the IRA rules is all that's needed to deal effectively with about 80 percent of all cases. And each person who inherits an IRA usually needs to know only some part of that 20 percent.

With that in mind, Parts 1 and 2 of my book have the "basics" that IRA inheritors need to know. But in Parts 3 and 4, there's a chapter for each of several different kinds of beneficiaries, so you'll only need one of those chapters. Finally, Part 5 has some advanced topics that may be of interest.

Here's a real life story of why you should be informed. Janet, along with her two siblings, each inherited part of an individual retirement account (IRA) from her father. Janet is married to Warren, who's one of the best estate planning lawyers I know. The IRA was held at an internationally renowned investment firm. Janet had an investment advisor at that firm, as well as a well-respected independent CPA. The investment advisor told Janet that she should withdraw the IRA immediately, because there was no real advantage to stretching distributions out over Janet's life expectancy. She didn't consult her CPA or her husband, Warren. Instead, Janet followed the investment's advisor's advice and made the withdrawal. Big mistake: that advice was wrong.

It turned out the advisor had prepared some rather complex computations. And those computations were significantly flawed.

Unfortunately, once that IRA had been emptied out, there was no way to restore it. Janet had to pay income taxes on all of her share of the IRA—all at once.

What is the moral of this true story? Some very competent professionals can get it wrong. Very wrong.

Here's what could have happened:

The IRA could have been divided into three Inherited IRAs (one for Janet and each of her siblings) by Dec. 31 of the year after their father died. Once that was done, each sibling could have taken annual withdrawals for many years, over each sibling's expected lifetime. This method of handling an Inherited IRA that has more than one beneficiary is found in tax regulations, as well as in IRS Publication 590. And, these types of steps are outlined in several books targeted to professionals, written about retirement benefits and IRAs, such as Natalie Choate's *Life and Death Planning for Retirement Benefits* (now in its seventh edition).

It's rather surprising who can get it wrong. In one of Natalie Choate's newsletters (called "Choate's Notes"), she devotes an entire page to her article, "Who Makes Retirement Benefit Mistakes?" She recounts real mistakes made by:

- The IRS
- Retirement plan administrators (the folks who run retirement plans for employers),
- Financial advisors and institutions,

…And finally, surprisingly …

- Natalie herself! (She claims she failed to refer to her own book before giving advice.)
- And, of course, I've made a mistake or two.

But what's a person who isn't an IRA expert to do? The answer is, arm yourself with information and ask questions, just as you'd do when dealing with any other important matter. Moreover, if you're looking for an IRA expert, you'll need to recognize who's an expert and who's not.

Bottom line: Make your Inherited IRA improve your overall financial picture. For example, you may need to use it to pay for education. Or, you might be launching a new business. Or, perhaps you have credit card debt that charges a high interest rate—so maybe it's best for you to use the Inherited IRA to rid yourself of all that interest, even if you have to pay income taxes on the IRA withdrawal to do that.

The goal? Create an overall financial plan to manage the many moving parts of your unique financial life. Understanding your Inherited IRA and what it has to offer should be one of the first steps in building the best financial plan for you.

PART 1

THE INHERITED IRA OPPORTUNITY

CHAPTER 1

Take Charge of Getting the Most Value from Your Inherited IRA

It's better to question than to make a mistake, so be patient with yourself; don't be afraid to ask for help; and don't let anyone rush you

To MAXIMIZE THE VALUE of your Inherited IRA and avoid costly mistakes, you should know:

- What makes IRAs different from other kinds of investment accounts
- Why it can be valuable to you to make withdrawals slowly, only as actually required
- Required withdrawal rules that apply to the particular IRA you inherited
- Whether you have the right to roll over the IRA to your own IRA
- How to protect and implement your rights
- Whether you should enlist the help of a professional

And be warned: It's my experience that there's a lot of misinformation even among highly qualified financial and legal professionals.

For example, you probably learned that you inherited an IRA when you received a letter from the financial institution (bank, trust company, investment firm, or life insurance company) that holds the

IRA. If that letter says you have to withdraw the entire IRA within five years, that letter might be wrong. I've seen that happen.

It's best to make your own determination as soon as possible about whether that letter is correct, because mistakes can cost you a lot, and often can't be fixed.

Remember, IRAs are provided by banks, trust companies, and other financial institutions that offer investments. Each has its own procedures and forms for dealing with IRAs. Seasoned IRA "experts" frequently have a difficult time wading through them. It's always better to question than to make a mistake, so be patient with yourself; don't be afraid to ask for help; and don't let anyone rush you.

CHAPTER 2
What's an IRA?

An IRA is a perfectly legal income tax shelter—but every time you make an IRA withdrawal, you shut down your IRA tax shelter just a little more

BEFORE YOU LEARN ANYTHING else, you should be clear about what exactly is an IRA. This chapter will introduce some of the important features of IRAs. While it's not meant to be an exhaustive description, it does provide enough information to get you acquainted.

An IRA can be any of a family of individual retirement accounts and individual retirement annuities. They are tax-favored bank accounts or investment accounts held by a financial institution (such as a bank, trust company, investment firm, or life insurance company).

An IRA Is a Perfectly Legal Income Tax Shelter

IRAs are authorized and regulated by the Internal Revenue Code (IRC).[1] Congress presumably created IRAs in the IRC to encourage taxpayers to save for retirement. But, what makes IRAs different from other kinds of investment accounts? Investment earnings from the IRA, like interest, dividends and capital gains, are sheltered from income taxes (although distributions to you from the IRA are generally taxable).[2] And, for many taxpayers, contributions to IRAs are tax-de-

---

1 See IRC § 408, for "traditional" IRAs; § 408A, for Roth IRAs.
2 IRC § 408(d), incorporating by reference § 72. See also, IRS Publication 590-B, distributions from Individual Retirement Arrangements (IRAs).

ductible.[3] Plus, some taxpayers qualify for a "saver's credit" by making contributions to IRAs (as well as to some other kinds of retirement accounts).[4] Thus, every time you make an IRA withdrawal, you shut down your IRA tax shelter—just a little more.

There Are Several Members of The IRA Cast of Characters That You Need to Be Familiar With

The IRA "creator" is the individual who makes regular contributions or rollover contributions of his or her own money (as opposed to inherited retirement funds) to his or her own IRA.

The "beneficiary" is you—that is, the person who is entitled to the IRA after the IRA creator dies.

The financial intuition that holds the IRA is the IRA "trustee" (when the financial institution is a bank or trust company and the IRA is a trust) or the IRA "custodian" (all other types of IRAs offered by financial institutions).

Distributions From Traditional IRAs Will Cost You Some Income Taxes

The amount of an IRA distribution that will be included in your taxable income is reduced by "basis."[5] Basis represents money in the IRA that has already been subjected to income taxes. "Basis" goes by several different names, such as "after-tax contributions," "investment in the account" or "investment in the contract."

If the IRA has basis, that's the part of the account you can withdraw tax-free. But you can't withdraw all of the tax-free part first and then make the IRS wait until later for its income taxes on the taxable part. Instead, you'll pay income taxes on part of each withdrawal.[6] The decedent's basis, if any, is found in the decedent's tax records and/or tax returns.[7]

---

3 IRC § 219 See also, IRS Publication 590-A, Contributions to Individual Retirement Arrangements (IRAs). An election may be made not be made to deduct contributions. § 219(f)(8). Nondeductible amounts are treated as additions to basis.
4 IRC § 25B.
5 IRC § 25B.
6 See IRS Publication 590-B.
7 To determine basis, obtain the IRA owner's most recent Form 8606, described in IRS Publication 590-B. Form 8606 is required to be filed, even if filing a U.S. individual tax return isn't required.

If the estate of the IRA creator had to pay estate taxes, you may qualify for an income tax deduction for a portion of the estate taxes. There's more on this topic in Chapter 23.

Your IRA withdrawals will be reported to you and to the IRS each year on IRS Form 1099-R ("Distributions From Pensions, Annuities, Retirement or Profit-Sharing Plans, IRAs, Insurance Contracts, etc."). You will receive a copy of that form in the mail soon after the end of the calendar year.

Distributions From Roth IRAs Might Not Cost You Any Income Taxes

All Roth IRA distributions are tax-free, if five years have lapsed since the Roth IRA creator first opened any Roth IRA.[8] That five years always begins on Jan. 1, even if the first Roth IRA contribution was made later in the year. For example, Jean established her first Roth IRA in 2010 at her Bank by making a $2,000 contribution. In 2014, she established another Roth IRA at an investment firm by making a $5,000 contribution. Both Roth IRAs will satisfy the five-year holding rule on Jan. 1, 2015.

Even within that five-year period, tax-free distributions are possible. That's because the Roth IRA's investment earnings are potentially taxable only when distributed to you, and those investment earnings get distributed last, by law.[9] Unlike traditional IRAs, regular contributions from Roth IRAs are withdrawn first, tax-free. Only after all of the tax-free part is withdrawn can there be taxable distributions of Roth IRA investment earnings.

IRAs Are Started by Making "Regular Contributions"

Contributions to traditional (non-Roth) IRAs may qualify for an income tax deduction (except for Roth IRA contributions), which makes it easier to accumulate savings.[10] But you may never make contributions to your Inherited IRA.[11]

---

8 IRC § 408A(d)(2)(B); Regs. § 1.408A-6, Q&A-2.
9 Regs. § 1.408A-6, Q&A-4.
10 Ibid, note 3.
11 Only the person who establishes IRA may make contributions. Regs. § 1.408-2.

You must have earned income, such as from a job or from self-employment, to make regular contributions to an IRA.[12] There's an annual ceiling on how much you may contribute.[13] For example, at the time this book was published, $5,500 may be contributed, and an additional $1,000 may be contributed if you're at least age 50, for a total of $6,500. The amount you contribute may be deducted on your income tax return up to an annual earned income limit, and depending on whether you or your spouse qualifies to participate in a retirement plan sponsored by an employer, for example, a 401(k) plan. The income tax deduction is reduced or eliminated based on how much income you or your spouse makes.[14] Limits on the income tax deduction just mean some or all of your contribution will be nondeductible.[15] You may still contribute up to $5,500 (plus another $1,000 if you're at least age 50).

For contributions to Roth IRAs only, your ability to contribute is limited or eliminated if your income exceeds certain levels.[16] There's no such limit on contributions to traditional IRAs.

IRAs May Also Accept a "Rollover Contribution"

Many retirement plan accounts held for employees, such as 401(k) accounts, can be rolled over to an IRA.[17] Rollovers are common after someone retires or leaves a job in which the employee had a retirement account.

IRA Accounts Have Contracts

The contract setting up and maintaining an IRA is a contract between the individual for whose benefit the IRA is held and the financial institution that offers the IRA. Many IRA providers call this contract an "IRA adoption agreement."

---

12 IRC § 219(b)(1)(B).

13 IRC § 4973 imposes an excise tax on contributions in excess of the maximum amount that may be for income tax purposes under § 219.

14 IRC § 219(g). See also, IRS Publication 590-B.

15 Nondeductible amounts are treated as additions to basis.

16 IRC § 408A(c)(3).

17 IRC § 402(c).

The Original IRA Creator May Designate a Beneficiary Who Will Receive the IRA After the Creator Dies

When an IRA creator dies, the IRA's beneficiary designation form (and not the IRA creator's will) controls who gets the IRA. If the IRA creator forgot to fill out the form designating a beneficiary, the IRA contract will specify a beneficiary. That varies from one financial institution to another. Often, that's either the decedent's estate (which IS controlled by the will, if there is one), the decedent's surviving spouse (if there is one), or the decedent's children (if there are any).

An Inherited IRA Is An IRA Set Up Especially For The Beneficiary Of A Decedent's IRA

That makes IRA income tax benefits available to the beneficiary, even though the beneficiary didn't make any IRA contributions. There's more on this topic in Chapter 4.

Every IRA Tax Shelter Will Be Shut Down on a Predetermined Schedule of "Required Minimum Distributions"

The tax laws force you to take distributions during your lifetime.[18] And there's a 50 percent penalty tax for failing to comply with those forced distributions–that's in addition to the income tax.[19] The pace of Required Minimum Distributions depends on who's the beneficiary.[20] For example, if you're the sole beneficiary, the pace is probably based on your age and IRS life expectancy tables (see Chapter 8). Because age and IRS life expectancy tables usually set the pace, an older beneficiary typically has to take Required Minimum Distributions faster than a younger beneficiary.

---

18 Such distributions are known as "required minimum distributions." IRC §§ 401(a)(9), 408(a)(6), relating to Individual Retirement Accounts, § 408(b)(3), relating to Individual Retirement Annuities. For this purpose, Roth IRAs are subject to Traditional IRA rules. § 408A(a). However, Required Minimum Distributions do not apply during the lifetime of the individual who makes Roth IRA contributions. § 408A(c)(5).

19 IRC § 4974. This penalty may be waived if it can be shown that the shortfall was due to reasonable error and that reasonable steps are being taken to remedy the shortfall. IRS Form 5329 must be filed to request the waiver, in the case of an IRA or Roth IRA.

20 IRC § 401(a)(9) related regulations are extensive and complex. Later chapters in this book describe how those rules apply when the death beneficiary of an IRA is an individual.

IRAs Can Invest in Anything, EXCEPT Life Insurance and Collectibles. But, It's OK to Invest in Certain Coins and Bullion

IRAs can't own collectibles, except for certain coins and bullion.[21] Ownership of anything on the prohibited list causes the collectible to be treated as having been distributed from the IRA.

Here's the list of prohibited collectibles:

- Any work of art
- Any rug or antique
- Any metal or gem
- Any stamp or coin
- Any alcoholic beverage (examples: collections of fine wines, beer, scotch and whiskey)

An IRA may hold coins and bullion, but those assets must be in the possession of the IRA trustee or custodian to qualify as exceptions to the prohibition on investing in collectibles. According to IRS Publication 590A (2014), Individual Retirement Arrangements (IRAs):

> Your IRA can invest in one, one-half, one-quarter, or one-tenth ounce U.S. gold coins, or one-ounce silver coins minted by the Treasury Department. It can also invest in certain platinum coins and certain gold, silver, palladium, and platinum bullion.

And the IRS also says: "An investment by an IRA in a coin which has been made into jewelry is still considered an investment in a collectible, and will be treated as a distribution."

No Loans or Pledges

Don't take a loan from your IRA or pledge it as collateral. That action will cause a taxable distribution to occur.[22]

---

21 IRC § 408(m). This section applies to both traditional and Roth IRAs. See also, IRS Publication 590A (2014), beginning at p. 34.

22 IRC § 408(d)(4)(A).

Instant IRA Killer: Prohibited Transactions

Engaging in acts of "self dealing" causes an IRA to terminate as of the first day of the year when the transaction occurs.[23] That means paying income taxes on the entire IRA, unless the IRA is a Roth IRA.

Prohibited transactions are transactions between your IRA and you or between your IRA and members of your family. It can sneak up on you. Say your IRA (or Inherited IRA) owns a condominium on Maui, Hawaii. Your daughter would like to stay there for two weeks. If she does that, that's considered a prohibited transaction (even if she pays rent). Worse: if you stay there to make repairs, or even if you make repairs yourself instead of hiring a contractor, that's also a prohibited transaction.

---

23 IRC § 4975. Generally, "prohibited transaction" means any direct or indirect-- (A) sale or exchange, or leasing, of any property between a plan and a disqualified person; (B) lending of money or other extension of credit between a plan and a disqualified person; (C) furnishing of goods, services, or facilities between a plan and a disqualified person; (D) transfer to, or use by or for the benefit of, a disqualified person of the income or assets of a plan; (E) act by a disqualified person who is a fiduciary whereby he deals with the income or assets of a plan in his own interest or for his own account; or (F) receipt of any consideration for his own personal account by any disqualified person who is a fiduciary from any party dealing with the plan in connection with a transaction involving the income or assets of the plan.

CHAPTER 3

A Lifetime of Paychecks: The Golden Rule of Inherited IRAs

*It's valuable to make withdrawals
only when actually required*

BEN FRANKLIN SAID THAT time is money, but there's nothing like having both money and time to grow it. If you pay taxes and can invest money over a significant period of time, an IRA (whether it's inherited or your own) makes you wealthier by allowing you to pay taxes later. Between now and the day when you do pay the taxes, you may invest the (temporarily) unpaid taxes for your own gain. A Roth IRA is even better than a traditional IRA because it's unlikely you'll ever have to pay income taxes on what's inside the Roth IRA, including investment earnings.

Traditional IRA Example

Let's say Sally inherits a traditional IRA worth $100,000, and that, if she withdraws all of it immediately, she will have $67,000 left after paying 33 percent in income taxes. Sally invests her remaining $67,000 for one year. She earns 8 percent on her investments, but earns 6 percent after paying income taxes at the rate of 25 percent on her investment earnings. At the end of the year, she will have $71,020.

Now, let's say that instead of withdrawing all of the IRA immediately, Sally waits one year. Because her withdrawal takes place after a year, the investment returns earned inside the IRA aren't subject to income taxes for that entire year. Let's also assume that Sally's IRA investments earned 8 percent inside the IRA during that year. After one year passes, the IRA is worth $108,000. When she withdraws the entire IRA after waiting one year, she will have $72,360 left after paying 33 percent in income taxes. Here's the score at the end of one year:

- $72,360 if she waits to withdraw the IRA
- But only $71,020 if she withdraws all of it immediately

Sally has $1,340 more, just by waiting one year to withdraw the IRA.

What if Sally could wait five years instead of one year? At the end of five years, and after income taxes are paid (assuming the same income tax rates and annual investment returns as applied when waiting one year), she would have:

- $98,445 if she waits to withdraw the IRA
- But only $89,661 if she withdraws all of it immediately

Waiting five years to withdraw the IRA is better by $8,784.

It gets even better if Sally can take distributions over her entire lifetime instead of within 5 years. In most cases, she can.

Example: Taking Traditional IRA Distributions Over Lifetime

Ron's mother, Catherine, dies, leaving her $300,000 IRA to Ron. Ron is evaluating two options. Option one is to withdraw the entire $300,000 immediately. Option two is to take Required Minimum Distributions over the next 21 years. Ron intends to invest all of his Inherited IRA distributions after paying income taxes.

Ron expects his investments to earn 6 percent before paying any income taxes and 4.5 percent after paying income taxes.

If he withdraws the entire IRA now, he'll pay $135,000 of income taxes (45 percent of $300,000). That will leave him $165,000 to invest. At the end of 21 years, he'll have $415,840.

But if Ron takes Required Minimum Distributions over 21 years, he'll have $586,341 at the end of 21 years. Stretching out distributions over 21 years gives Ron $170,501 more than cashing out the IRA, an increase of 41 percent. That's equivalent to adding $67,653 to the $165,000 value of cashing out now. Computations supporting this example are in Appendix A.

Roth IRA Example

Roth IRA inheritors must take Required Minimum Distributions even though the Roth IRA owner didn't have to.

What happens to the one-year Inherited IRA example (Sally) if the IRA is a tax-free Roth IRA instead of a traditional IRA? If Sally withdraws all of it immediately, she'll have $100,000 to invest for the next year. Her annual investment earnings after paying income taxes will still be 6 percent, causing her money to grow to $106,000 at the end of that year. But if she waits one year to withdraw the Roth IRA, she will have $108,000, because Sally pays no income tax on the 8 percent investment earnings inside the Roth IRA. That's a $2,000 improvement. Here's the score at the end of one year:

- Sally will have $108,000 if she waits to withdraw the Roth IRA
- But only $106,000 if she withdraws all of it immediately

Sally has $2,000 more, just by waiting one year to withdraw the Roth IRA.

What if Sally could wait five years instead of one year? At the end of five years:

- Sally will have $146,933 if she waits to withdraw the Roth IRA
- But only $133,823 if she withdraws all of it immediately

With a Roth IRA, waiting is better by $13,110.

It gets even better if Sally can take distributions over her entire lifetime instead of within five years. In most cases, she can.

Example: Taking Roth IRA Distributions Over Lifetime

Ron's mother, Catherine, dies, leaving her $300,000 Roth IRA to Ron. Ron is evaluating two options. Option one is to withdraw the entire $300,000 immediately. Option two is to take Required Minimum Distributions over the next 21 years. Ron intends to invest all of his Roth Inherited IRA distributions after paying income taxes.

Ron expects his investments to earn 6 percent before paying any income taxes and 4.5 percent after paying income taxes.

If he withdraws the entire Roth IRA now, he'll pay no of income taxes. That will leave him $300,000 to invest. At the end of 21 years, he'll have $756,072.

But if Ron takes Required Minimum Distributions over 21 years, he'll have $875,135 at the end of 21 years. Stretching out distributions over 21 years gives Ron $119,063 more than cashing out the Roth IRA, an increase of over 15 percent. That's equivalent to adding $47,243 to the $300,000 value of cashing out now. Computations supporting this example are in Appendix B.

How the Waiting Advantage Works

You probably get the idea by now: An IRA is likely to be worth more, the longer you wait to make withdrawals, even after paying income taxes (assuming that your investments grow and that you remain in the same income tax bracket.)

Here's why: You get a financial boost from the difference between the nontaxable rate of return earned inside the IRA (8 percent in our example) versus the net taxable rate of return earned outside the IRA (6 percent in our example). The bigger that difference is, the more money you make by leaving money inside the IRA for as long as allowed.

If it looks like your income tax rates will go up, should you withdraw the IRA? Not necessarily. If you expect your tax rate to be higher later, it seems like that can work against you, but it might still make waiting highly valuable. This is because the difference increases between the nontaxable rate of return earned inside the IRA versus the net taxable rate of return earned outside the IRA. That's where careful analysis is needed.

Required Minimum Distributions Equals Your Lifetime of Paychecks

Of course, Congress knows what a great thing it can be to pay taxes later instead of sooner, so they force you to take withdrawals at some point. These forced withdrawals are the Required Minimum Distributions. In many (not all) Inherited IRAs, Required Minimum Distributions can be taken slowly, over your life expectancy. It's like getting a lifetime of paychecks. (See Chapter 8.)

So, waiting to make IRA withdrawals can have enormous value. *But beware: some IRA custodians or trustees might mistakenly tell you that you have to take Required Minimum Distributions out sooner than you actually have to.*

If you want the most value out of your Inherited IRA, you must take charge of making Required Minimum Distributions happen correctly. If you are planning to save your Required Minimum Distributions, consider using them to fund your own retirement accounts. For more on this strategy, see Chapter 24.

CHAPTER 4

What's an Inherited IRA?

Individual beneficiaries may have an Inherited IRA;
Surviving Spouses may also make a rollover

Your Inherited IRA

"INHERITED IRA" MEANS THE IRA of a decedent that's been set up for that IRA's death beneficiary. It usually has up to two names on its title: (1) the name of the decedent who made lifetime contributions to the IRA (its original creator), and (2) the name of the beneficiary who inherited it. Other, similar terms are "beneficiary IRA" and "decedent's IRA."

For example, William Johnson's IRA, containing assets that William accumulated when he was alive, had his name on it. William named his daughter, Samantha, as the beneficiary of his IRA. After William died, Samantha opened up a new Inherited IRA. The title on the Inherited IRA became: "IRA of William Johnson, deceased, for the benefit of Samantha Johnson." (In practice, "FBO" is often used to abbreviate "for the benefit of.") Note that there are variations on titles of Inherited IRAs, such as the title may be, "Samantha Johnson Inherited IRA."

In most cases, you can't get access to your inheritance until after you open your Inherited IRA. You'll probably have to do what Samantha Johnson did: move the investments from the IRA that has only the decedent's name on it, into an IRA that adds your name on to the account, along with the decedent's name (called an "Inherited IRA" or a "beneficiary IRA"). To open your Inherited IRA, you'll have to sign a document, usually called an "IRA adoption agreement". But beware: IRA adoption agreements differ from one custodian to the next. It therefore pays to read and understand the contract before you agree to its terms. And, be sure to name a beneficiary who will receive your Inherited IRA upon your death.

Trusts

If the Inherited IRA is held in a trust (meaning that a trust was the IRA's death beneficiary) and you are a beneficiary of that trust, you might be able to move it to an Inherited IRA, provided you're entitled to the trust's Inherited IRA under the terms of the trust. You'll need to consult an attorney to determine what rights you may have.

Surviving Spouses Only

A surviving spouse is the only person who may roll over or make a direct transfer of a decedent's IRA to one that has only the spouse's name on the IRA's title and not the decedent's.[1] If the surviving spouse does make a rollover or transfer, the decedent's IRA is transformed into an IRA of the surviving spouse.[2] From that point on, it's just as if the surviving spouse never inherited the IRA, but instead accumulated it by making her own contributions–so it's no longer an Inherited IRA.

An Inherited IRA of a surviving spouse is helpful instead of a rollover when the surviving spouse needs to avoid a 10 percent tax on distributions made before the surviving spouse has attained age 59½.[3] If the surviving spouse chooses to do this, all rules that apply to any non-spouse IRA beneficiary will apply to the surviving spouse.

The surviving spouse isn't stuck with an Inherited IRA for life. The surviving spouse can choose to make a spousal rollover or direct transfer to a spousal rollover account at any time, even years later.[4]

---

1 IRC § 408(d)(3)(C).

2 IRC § 408(d)(3)(C)(ii)(II).

3 IRC § 72(t)(2)(a)(ii).

4 Regs. § 1.408-8, Q&A-5 provides that a surviving spouse may elect to treat an IRA of the deceased spouse as an IRA of the surviving spouse at any time.

CHAPTER 5

Opening an Inherited IRA and Transferring IRA Assets

Always remember this warning: IRA money in motion is IRA money at risk. Here's your roadmap to avoiding big mistakes

WHETHER YOU'RE THE ONLY IRA beneficiary or one of several beneficiaries, it's likely you can make a transfer to your own Inherited IRA that you manage and control.

Whatever you do, don't let the IRA provider that has the decedent's IRA write a check made out to you (except for the decedent's final year Required Minimum Distribution). That's a complete disaster if you're not the decedent's surviving spouse: it means the end of your Inherited IRA![1] And, almost always, it can't be fixed (rarely, it can be fixed if it was a mistake that the IRA provider made).[2]

The right way to move funds (including investments held in the decedent's IRA) is by direct, trustee-to-trustee transfer. That means

---

1 An Inherited IRA is a continuation of the decedent's IRA. But, instead of being held for the benefit of the decedent, it's held for the benefit of the death beneficiary. In practice, the IRA that existed while the decedent was still living is closed, and its funds are transferred to an Inherited IRA.

2 The decedent's IRA terminates when a check is issued to the IRA's death beneficiary instead of being transferred to an IRA of the decedent held for the benefit of that beneficiary. The death beneficiary can't make a rollover, unless the beneficiary is the decedent's surviving spouse. IRC § 408(d)(3)(C).

that funds and/or investments move directly from the decedent's IRA to your Inherited IRA without passing through your hands.[3]

If you're the surviving spouse and a check was made payable to you, you can make a rollover within 60 days of when you received the distribution. You can't make a rollover to an Inherited IRA, but you can make a rollover to an IRA held in your own name (see Chapter 12).[4]

There are three steps you must take to set up an Inherited IRA. (Note that this doesn't apply to a spousal rollover.)

Step 1: Withdraw (or finish withdrawing) the decedent's Required Minimum Distribution, if the decedent didn't,

Step 2: Open an Inherited IRA, and

Step 3: Move the assets directly from the decedent's IRA to the Inherited IRA in a "trustee-to-trustee transfer." There should be no IRA check made out that's payable to you or to any account that's **not** an IRA!

Step 1: Withdraw the Decedent's Required Minimum Distribution, if the Decedent Didn't

Take this step on time (if required) or pay a 50 percent penalty on the late Required Minimum Distribution.[5] If the IRA creator died on or after a date called the "Required Beginning Date", a distribution was supposed to be made before Dec. 31 in the year of death. [6]You will have to withdraw whatever part of that Required Minimum Distribution the IRA creator didn't withdraw.

---

3 Direct transfers enable Inherited IRA mobility because direct transfers are not rollovers. Direct transfers are recognized in Rev. Rul. 78-406, 1978-2 C.B. 157. In that ruling, a distribution from an IRA held at "bank X" was made to its owner in 1976, then rolled over to a second IRA held at "bank Y". In 1977, bank Y transferred the funds from the bank Y IRA to a new IRA at set up at "bank Z." The IRS held that "the transfer of the IRA from trustee bank Y to trustee bank Z did not result in a payment or distribution includible in the gross income of the participant."

4 IRC § 408(d)(3)(C)(ii)(II).

5 IRC § 4974. The penalty may be waived under certain circumstances.

6 IRC § 401(a)(9). An IRA owner's first Required Minimum Distribution is a distribution with respect to the year when IRA owner attained age 70½. That distribution is due by the Required Beginning Date. The second Required Minimum Distribution is a distribution with respect to the year when the Required Beginning Date occurs. That second distribution is due by December 31 of the year when the Required Beginning Date occurs.

EXAMPLE: Zoe died June 25, 2013, during a year when her Required Minimum Distribution was $6,000. Zoe had set up automatic distributions of $500 on the 15th of each month in 2013 to meet her obligation to make those distributions. By the time she died, only $3,000 had been distributed. Max, the IRA beneficiary, must withdraw $3,000 by Dec. 31, 2013. The IRA custodian won't automatically do this, so Max must initiate the withdrawal himself.

The Required Beginning Date for an IRA creator is April 1 of the year after the year when the IRA creator turns age 70½.[7] To learn more about what Required Minimum Distributions are and how to find the Required Beginning Date, read Chapter 8 and Chapter 9.

Step 2: Open the Inherited IRA

You'll need to open an Inherited IRA to receive the assets in the decedent's IRA, unless you plan to withdraw the entire IRA.

What Can Go Wrong?

The decedent's IRA will be completely and immediately taxable if the IRA's assets wind up in a non-IRA account.[8] The same tax disaster will occur if a check is made out to you and not to an Inherited IRA (unless you're the IRA creator's surviving spouse). Unlike with your own IRA, you don't have 60 days to roll over the assets into any other IRA, including an Inherited IRA.[9] If the assets wind up in an IRA that doesn't mention that it was inherited by you, it's your own IRA, not an Inherited IRA. Unless you're the IRA creator's surviving spouse, two very unfortunate things will happen: (1) the IRA that you inherited will be completely and immediately taxable,[10] and (2) you've made an impermissible "excess" contribution to your own IRA, which will cost you a 6 percent tax penalty every year until you remove the funds

---

7 Regs. § 1.408-8, Q&A-3.

8 IRC § 408(d).

9 IRC § 408(d)(3)(C).

10 An IRA that is distributed but not rolled over is taxable under the general rule of IRC 408(d).

from the IRA.[11] You can avoid the penalty by taking the money and all income earned on the impermissible contribution out of the account before the due date (including extensions) of your income tax return for the year when the mistake occurred.[12]

Your Cover Letter

You will have to submit forms to the IRA custodian to transfer the decedent's IRA into your Inherited IRA. To reduce the chances of making a critical mistake, give the forms to your financial advisor, along with a cover letter that says what you're trying to do. For example:

> Dear Bobby Markets,
>
> Before you submit my forms for processing, please review the enclosed forms and let me know if the forms need to be changed to achieve my goal.
>
> My goal is to transfer, in a direct trustee-to-trustee transfer, all of my share of the Richard E. Jones IRA to an Inherited IRA set up and maintained for my benefit, so that I may take required minimum distributions over my lifetime.
>
> Yours truly,
>
> Jean Smith

What to Watch Out For

The paperwork needed to set up your Inherited IRA can be confusing. Have a professional advisor whom you trust help you fill out the forms. I've found some of the forms confusing and difficult to use, and I'm a CPA who has seen lots of forms from lots of IRA custodians. I often need to ask the IRA custodian questions before those forms get submitted.

---

11 IRC § 4973.
12 IRC § 4973(b), flush language.

Here's some advice: Don't do it online. Irreversible disaster can be just a click away! Check one wrong box online and your Inherited IRA will end abruptly, costing you immediate income taxes. Instead, use the old-fashioned paper forms that you can check over carefully and that you can have someone else check over carefully. It's fine to download forms available online—just don't fill them out and submit them in a single online session.

The forms are usually part of a booklet, which, if you sign it and submit it, will become a legal agreement between you and the IRA provider (meaning the IRA trustee or the IRA custodian, as the case may be.) Not all IRA agreements are alike. It's a good idea to read them in their entirety, even though they are lengthy. You'll need to sign the forms and agree to the provider's contract terms to open your Inherited IRA.

When you fill out the forms in the booklet, you'll be asked who your beneficiary will be. In other words, if you die while your Inherited IRA has assets, who will get your Inherited IRA? Be thoughtful about this. Naming a beneficiary is part of your overall estate plan. If you have an estate-planning advisor, review the IRA beneficiary form with him or her before you sign it, because IRAs will pass upon your death directly to the beneficiary you name—your will or revocable living trust will not automatically control who gets your Inherited IRA (or your own IRA, if you have one).

If you don't name a beneficiary, the IRA agreement will specify who will inherit it from you. Sometimes, this information is printed on the beneficiary form; other times, it's in the fine print somewhere else in the booklet.

Ask your Inherited IRA custodian what the title will say. An Inherited IRA will have your name on the title, but also will indicate that the IRA was inherited (in contrast to being an IRA of your own that you make contributions to). Examples of how title of an Inherited IRA looks are:

- Philip Reese IRA, deceased fbo Paul Reese
- Paul Reese Beneficiary IRA
- Paul Reese Inherited IRA

Step 3: Moving the Assets Directly From the Decedent's IRA to the Inherited IRA

IRA money in motion is IRA money at risk. IRA custodians sometimes make mistakes when they process the forms that establish Inherited IRAs. This type of mistake is out of your control, except to the extent you can catch a mistake very early by monitoring the progress of your forms processing very closely.

The Goal Is a Direct Transfer to an Inherited IRA

To make a direct transfer, you might need to fill out another set of forms in addition to those that established the Inherited IRA. This second set of forms empties out the decedent's IRA and moves its funds into your Inherited IRA. Most IRA custodians use a form called a "withdrawal" form or a "distribution" form.

Your goal in filling out these forms is to make the IRA assets pass directly from the account you inherited (the decedent's IRA that named you as beneficiary), to the Inherited IRA that has your name on it. Look for a place on the form that provides for for a direct transfer to another IRA. Some forms call this a "direct transfer," while others call it a "direct rollover." It's called "direct" because the IRA contents never move outside an IRA. If you see or hear this term, confirm that the contents of the decedent's IRA will get to your Inherited IRA in only one step that's direct and nonstop from one IRA account to the other. In other words, there should be no IRA check made out that's payable to you or to any account that's not an IRA.

CHAPTER 6

Do It Yourself or Hire an Expert?

It's up to you

DOING IT YOURSELF OBVIOUSLY is cheaper than hiring and paying an expert. On the other hand, it's all so complicated that it's very easy to make a costly mistake. By analogy, even the most experienced professionals normally seek review before making recommendations to clients. When it comes to an Inherited IRA, it's best not to venture alone into unfamiliar territory when the cost of a misstep is so high.

Hiring an expert lowers the risk of making a dreadful error. But it's also true that no one, not even a paid expert, cares about this process like you do. That's why it works best to team up with an expert for guidance, while staying in charge of the process.

Your first task is to learn what your rights are, and you've started by picking up this book. If you want assistance, shop for a professional who has knowledge and a history of success in working with Inherited IRAs.

Specifically, ask the individual you're considering whether you can rely on his or her tax advice. For example, many IRA custodians prefer not to give tax advice, and their forms typically indicate that you're not entitled to rely on them for such advice.

Whether you seek outside assistance, at minimum, here are some items you'll need to gather:

- A copy of the beneficiary form (if you have access to that)
- The name and date of birth of each IRA beneficiary
- If the beneficiary is a trust, a copy of the trust
- The dates of the IRA creator's birth and death (you may be asked for a copy of the death certificate)
- Forms from your IRA custodian or trustee for setting up your inherited or spousal IRA
- Forms from the IRA custodian or trustee of the decedent's IRA for transferring the decedent's IRA to the Inherited IRA
- Names, social security numbers and dates of birth of the individuals you wish to name as beneficiaries of your Inherited IRA, in case you die while there are still investments in your Inherited IRA. (Alternatively, you may wish to set up a trust for these beneficiaries.)
- Full legal names and addresses of charities you wish to name as beneficiaries of your Inerhited IRA.

CHAPTER 7

Important Deadlines

After an IRA creator dies, these are deadlines with consequences

Year of death, by Dec. 31.

Withdraw the IRA creator's Required Minimum Distribution for the year of death that the IRA creator didn't withdraw before death. The distribution is paid to the beneficiary (or beneficiaries) of the IRA. See Chapter 9.

Within nine months of the IRA creator's date of death,

Anyone who wishes to refuse to accept any portion of the IRA must make a qualified disclaimer. See Chapter 26.

Year after death, by Sept. 30.

Distribute the entire share of each IRA beneficiary who will cause Required Minimum Distributions to be made in a very short time. For example: a charity. See Chapter 10.

Year after death, by Apr. 15 (or Oct. 15 by extending the due date of the decedent's tax return) - last possible date for:

- Recharacterizing a decedent's Roth IRA conversion during the year of death to a traditional IRA (thereby negating all tax effects of the Roth IRA conversion)
- Recharacterizing a decedent's regular traditional IRA contribution in the year of death to Roth IRA contribution
- Recharacterizing a decedent's regular Roth IRA contribution in the year of death to regular IRA contribution
- (See Chapter 28.)

Year after death, by Oct. 31.

If a trust is beneficiary of the IRA and a trust beneficiary's age is meant to pace the Required Minimum Distributions, the IRA trustee or custodian must be provided with either a copy of the trust or a certified list of trust beneficiaries. See Chapter 10.

Year after death, by Dec. 31.

Required Minimum Distributions must begin for IRAs and Roth IRAs, unless the five-year rule applies. In some cases, failure to meet this deadline causes the five-rule to apply. See Chapter 8.

Year after death, by Dec. 31.

If there are multiple beneficiaries who each could qualify for stretching distributions out over life expectancy, establish one Inherited IRA for each so that each beneficiary can set his or her own pace for making Required Minimum Distributions. The decedent's IRA must be transferred to the Inherited IRAs by Dec. 31 of the year after the year the IRA creator died. See Chapter 11.

PART 2

INHERITED IRA-SPEAK

CHAPTER 8

What Are Required Minimum Distributions?

You must withdraw Required Minimum Distributions each year
In most cases, you may withdraw more than is required

CONGRESS KNOWS WHAT A great thing waiting to withdraw an IRA is, so, they make you take withdrawals called Required Minimum Distributions.[1] You may withdraw more than is required, but you can't withdraw less.

It's up to you to figure out how much each year's Required Minimum Distribution is; it's also up to you to withdraw it.

Fortunately, the rules that apply most often to most IRA inheritors can be summarized briefly (relatively speaking), and that's what this chapter will do. More details about how Required Minimum Distributions apply to specific IRA inheritors are in subsequent chapters of this book.

Planning to save or invest your Required Minimum Distributions? Consider using them to fund your own retirement accounts. (For more, read Chapter 24.)

Many IRA inheritors consider getting help from an experienced professional. But even if you get help, do your best to under-

---

1 IRC §§ 401(a)(9), 403(b)(10), 408(a)(6), 408(b)(3), or 457(d)(2).

stand the rules so you can tell whether the advice you get is correct and complete.

50 Percent Penalty

The government is serious about this: there's a 50 percent penalty on the failure to take Required Minimum Distributions.[2] IRS Form 5329, which sports the catchy title "Additional Taxes Attributable to IRAs, Other Qualified Retirement Plans, Annuities, Modified Endowment Contracts and MSAs", must be attached to your income tax return to report and pay the penalty. See Chapter 22 for more information, but here are a couple of quick examples.

> EXAMPLE: Earl was required to withdraw $8,000 during 2012, but he didn't do it. Earl owes a penalty of $4,000.

> EXAMPLE: Gracie was required to withdraw $8,000 during 2012, but she only withdrew $6,000. She owes a $1,000 penalty on the $2,000 shortfall.

The tax law says the IRS may waive the penalty if there's a good reason why there was a shortfall, and you're taking reasonable steps to remedy it.[3] A common example is if you relied on a qualified professional who should have known enough to advise you about Required Minimum Distributions, but failed to do so. Before asking for the penalty waiver, each late Required Minimum Distribution should be withdrawn. See Chapter 22 for more information.

Required Minimum Distribution Basics

Required Minimum Distributions work like this: Every year, the amount equal to the value of the IRA is divided by the life expectancy of a Designated Beneficiary (if there is one). The life expectancy is called an "Applicable Distribution Period"[4] in the IRS regulations and is found in one of three IRS tables.

> EXAMPLE: A Required Minimum Distribution must be made for calendar year 2013. The value of the account

2 IRC § 4974.
3 IRC § 4974(d).
4 Reg. § 1.401(a)(9)-5, Q&A-1(a).

is $100,000 on Dec. 31, 2012, and the Applicable Distribution Period is 34.2 years. The 2013 Required Minimum Distribution is $2,923.98 ($100,000 divided by 34.2).

IRA inheritors use the "Single Life Table".[5] Living IRA creators use the "Uniform Lifetime Table",[6] with the following exception. A living IRA creator may use the "Joint and Last Survivor Table" instead of the Uniform Lifetime Table if the IRA creator's spouse is the only IRA beneficiary and the spouse was born more than 10 calendar years later than the IRA creator.[7] (It turns out that marrying a much younger spouse reduces Required Minimum Distributions, especially late in life.) The tables are found in IRS Publication 590, available on the IRS website (http://www.irs.gov/pub/irs-pdf/p590.pdf). The Uniform Lifetime Table is reproduced in Appendix C, and the Single Life Table is reproduced in Appendix D.

Here's how the three tables compare, ranking them from the one that causes the smallest Required Minimum Distributions to the table that causes the largest, for a given age:

- Joint and Last Survivor Table
- Uniform Lifetime Table
- Single Life Table

Required Minimum Distribution rules are described in detail in IRS regulations.[8] The regulations are long because they have to be, and it's mind numbing to read them – even for a tax nerd.

Do You Also Have Your Own IRA?

If you have your own IRA in addition to an Inherited IRA, the rules about Required Minimum Distributions will apply differently to your own IRA than they will to your Inherited IRA. You may not combine your Inherited IRA and your own IRA into one IRA[9], unless you're the surviving spouse of the IRA creator. For example, if you have

5 Reg. § 1.401(a)(9)-5, Q&A-5(a) and (c).
6 Reg. § 1.401(a)(9)-5, Q&A-4(a).
7 Reg. § 1.401(a)(9)-5, Q&A-4(b).
8 For traditional IRAs, Reg. § 1.408-8, Q&A-1 generally adopts Reg. §§ 1.401(a)(9)-1 through 1.401(a)(9)-9; § 1.408-8; For Roth IRAs, see Reg. § 1.408A-6.
9 IRC § 408(d)(3)(C).

not reached your own Required Beginning Date, you will not have to start taking Required Minimum Distributions from your own IRA just because you have to start taking distributions from your Inherited IRA. Also, while you will be required to use the Single Life Table[10] for your Inherited IRA's Required Minimum Distributions, you will not use that table for your own IRA. Instead, use the Uniform Lifetime Table.[11] If you're married, your spouse is the only beneficiary of the IRA and she was born more than 10 calendar years after you, you may use the Joint and Last Survivor Table.[12]

The Year When the IRA Creator Dies

There may be a Required Minimum Distribution in the year of the IRA creator's death that wasn't withdrawn during lifetime. If so, that Required Minimum Distribution must be withdrawn by Dec. 31 of the year of the IRA creator's death. To learn more, read Chapter 9.

Three Options

There are three methods for Required Minimum Distributions from an Inherited IRA:

1. *The five-year rule.* The entire account must be distributed by Dec. 31 of the year containing the fifth anniversary of the IRA creator's death[13] (a not very good option);

2. *The life expectancy method.* Distributions are made over either the life expectancy of an individual beneficiary or what would have been the remaining life expectancy of the decedent, whichever is longer[14] (a better option); and

3. *The surviving spouse rollover.* The decedent's IRA becomes an IRA of the surviving spouse (usually – but not always –the best option).[15]

---

10 Reg. § 1.401(a)(9)-5, Q&A-5(a) and (c). The Single Life Table is located at Reg. § 1.401(a)(9)-9, Q&A-1, and is reproduced in APPENDIX D of this book.

11 Reg. § 1.401(a)(9)-5, Q&A-4. The Uniform Lifetime Table is located at Reg. § 1.401(a)(9)-9, Q&A-2, and is reproduced in APPENDIX C of this book.

12 Reg. § 1.401(a)(9)-5, Q&A-4(b)(1). The Joint and Last Survivor Table is located at Reg. § 1.401(a)(9)-9, Q&A-3, and is reproduced in APPENDIX C of this book.

13 IRC § 401(a)(9)(B)(ii).

14 IRC § 401(a)(9)(B)(iii).

15 IRC § 408(d)(3)(A) and (C).

The IRA Creator's Required Beginning Date Makes a Difference

How the three methods work depends on whether the IRA creator died before reaching the date when he had to begin taking lifetime Required Minimum Distributions. This date is called the "Required Beginning Date".[16]

Here's a timeline that shows which methods are available. Note that that the five-year rule applies only when the IRA creator's death occurs before the Required Beginning Date:

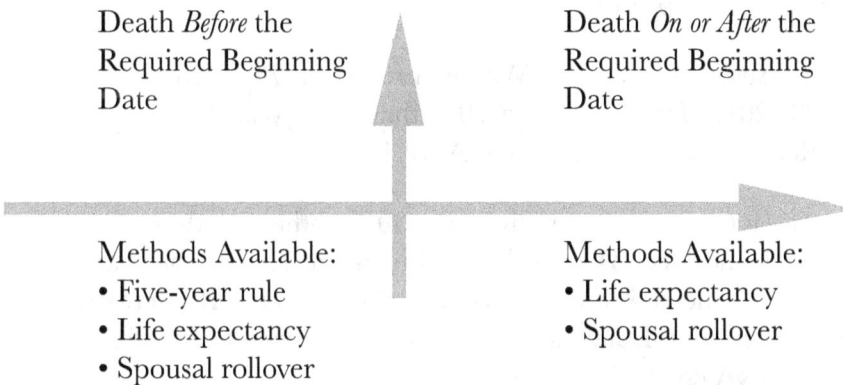

Death *Before* the Required Beginning Date	Death *On or After* the Required Beginning Date
Methods Available:	Methods Available:
• Five-year rule	• Life expectancy
• Life expectancy	• Spousal rollover
• Spousal rollover	

The IRA Creator's Required Beginning Date

Inherited Roth IRAs must make Required Minimum Distributions even though the Roth IRA owner didn't have to.[17] Because Roth IRAs have no Required Minimum Distributions during the Roth IRA creator's lifetime, death always occurs before the Roth IRA creator's Required Beginning Date.[18]

For a traditional (non-Roth) IRA creator, the Required Beginning Date is April 1 of the year after the year during which the IRA creator reaches age 70½.[19]

The Required Beginning Date can be tricky because age 70½ sometimes falls in the same year as the 70th birthday, but sometimes it falls in the following year.

---

16 IRC § 401(a)(9)(C).
17 IRC § 408(c)(5).
18 Reg. § 1.408A-6, Q&A-14(b).
19 Reg. § 1.408-8, Q&A-3.

An IRA creator who dies at age 72 or older has died after reaching the Required Beginning Date.

An IRA creator who dies at age 70 or younger has died before reaching the Required Beginning Date.

An IRA creator who dies at age 71 might or might not have died before reaching the Required Beginning Date. Here's how to tell. An IRA creator born before July 1 (in other words, born between Jan. 1 and June 30 inclusive) turns age 70½ in the same year as the year of the IRA creator's 70th birthday. So, the IRA creator's Required Beginning Date will be April 1 of the first year after the year of the IRA creator's 70th birthday.

> EXAMPLE: IRA creator Wilbur turned age 70 on May 29, 2012. He turned age 70½ that same year, so his Required Beginning Date is April 1, 2013.

An IRA creator born after June 30 (in other words, born between July 1 and Dec. 31 inclusive) will turn age 70½ in the year after the year of the IRA creator's 70th birthday. So the IRA creator's Required Beginning Date will be April 1 of the second year after the year of the IRA creator's 70th birthday.

> EXAMPLE: IRA creator Penny was born on Aug. 2, 1940. She turned age 70 on Aug. 2, 2010. She turned age 70½ during 2011 (on Feb.2, 2011), so her Required Beginning Date is April 1, 2012 (April 1 of the year after she turned 70½). If Penny dies during 2012 on or before Mar. 31, she will be 71 years old, but she will have died before reaching her Required Beginning Date.

Here's a handy worksheet for determining the Required Beginning Date for the IRA creator from whom you inherited your IRA, using Penny as an example:

Enter the year of the IRA creator's birth	1940
Add 70	70
If born on or after July 1, add (1)	1
Enter the total of the above numbers. Age 70 1/2 is reached in the year	2011
Enter the next year. The Required Beginning Dare is April 1 of this year.	2012

Now compare the Required Beginning Date to the date of the IRA creator's death. Did the IRA creator die before reaching the Required Beginning Date? (If the IRA creator died ON the Required Beginning Date, the answer is "no".)[20]

Is There More Than One IRA?

If you inherited several IRAs from the same person, you may consolidate them into a single Inherited IRA. On the other hand, if you choose to maintain several Inherited IRAs, you must compute the Required Minimum Distribution separately for each of those IRAs.[21] You may choose to take any or all of the Required Minimum Distribution of one IRA from any other that you inherit from the same IRA creator. [22]For example, if you inherited two IRAs from one IRA creator, you may add together the Required Minimum Distributions of both, and take the total from just one of the IRAs. That can be a help, for instance, when one IRA has investments that are difficult to turn into cash and, at the same time, another IRA has investments that are more liquid.

The Five-Year Rule

This is almost always the worst distribution rule after death.

If the five-year rule applies to you, the entire IRA must be emptied out by Dec. 31 of the year that's five years after the IRA creator's death.[23] You get an extra year if the IRA creator died during any year beginning Jan.1, 2004 and ending through Dec. 31, 2009, be-

---

20 Reg. § 1.401(a)(9)-3, Q&A-1.
21 Reg. § 1.401(a)(9)-5, Q&A-4(b).
22 Reg. § 1.408-8, Q&A-9. 1.408A-6, Q&A-14.
23 Reg. § 1.401(a)(9)-3, Q&A-2.

cause Congress passed a one-year moratorium of Required Minimum Distributions for 2009.[24]

> EXAMPLE: Alfred died in 2010. If the five-year rule applies, Alfred's IRA must be emptied out by Dec. 31, 2015.

> EXAMPLE: Abigail died in 2009. If the five-rule applies, her IRA must be emptied out by Dec. 31, 2015. There's an extra year because Abigail died between 2004 and 2009, the time frame that contained the one-year moratorium.

Fortunately, the five-year rule applies only if the IRA creator died before reaching the IRA creator's require beginning date and either:

- The five-year rule is mandatory under the custodian's own rules,
- OR it was elected by either you or the IRA creator,
- OR the beneficiary was not an individual. For example, the IRA creator's estate was the IRA beneficiary.

The good news is that most IRA custodians let you make the choice, unless #3 applies. Some IRAs specify lifetime Required Minimum Distributions and rule out use of the 5-year rule, unless there was no beneficiary that will qualify for lifetime Required Minimum Distributions. If the IRA document is completely silent on whether the 5-year rule does or does not apply, IRS regulations fill in the blank: the life expectancy method must be used if there is a qualifying Designated Beneficiary.[25]

Now the bad news: you can elect it without knowing you elected it. That can (but doesn't necessarily) happen if you don't start taking distributions by Dec. 31 of the year after the IRA creator died. You're protected if either the IRA documents specify lifetime Required Minimum Distributions and rules out use of the 5-year rule or if the

---

24 IRC § 401(a)(9)(H), Repealed. Pub. L. 113-295, title II, Sec. 221(a)(52), Dec. 19, 2014, 128 Stat. 4045. The repeal was not retroactive; rather, the provision was "deadwood" by 2014.

25 Reg. § 1.401(a)(9)-3, Q&A-4.

IRA documents are silent, unless there was no beneficiary that will qualify for lifetime Required Minimum Distributions.

Figuring out if the five-year rule applies to you means digging into the written IRA documents (these are legal documents). It's usually found in the IRA adoption agreement, but sometimes the IRA provider has a separate document called a "plan".

Don't rely on letters or summaries from the IRA provider. Sometimes IRA providers hand out erroneous information. Go right to the actual IRA documents and keep digging and asking until you find what you need.

Applying the Life Expectancy Method

The life expectancy method lets you take Required Minimum Distributions over your lifetime if you were the only IRA beneficiary. But if the IRA creator died on or after reaching the Required Beginning Date and that IRA creator's single life expectancy under the Single Life Table would have been longer, you may use that lifetime instead. (In other words, the IRA creator was younger than you.)[26]

The amount of the distribution is the value of the account at the beginning of the calendar year[27], divided by the life expectancy of a "Designated Beneficiary." Chapter 10 discusses what's meant by "Designated Beneficiary" – it's not always the same thing as "IRA beneficiary."[28]

If you're the only beneficiary and you're the surviving spouse of the IRA creator, the method for making distributions is in Chapter 14. You may also be able to make it your own IRA. That's covered in Chapters 12 and 15

If you're an individual (in other words, a human being as opposed to, say, an estate), you're the only beneficiary, and you aren't the surviving spouse of the IRA creator, the method for making distributions is outlined in Chapter 16.

If there's more than one beneficiary, the method for identifying the Designated Beneficiary (and whether there is a Designated Beneficiary) is outlined in Chapter 10.

---

26 Reg. § 1.401(a)(9)-5, Q&A-5(a).

27 Reg. § 1.401(a)(9)-5, Q&A-1(a).

28 Reg. §§ 1.408-8, Q&A-6 through 8; § 1.401(a)(9)-5, Q&A-3.

If there's more than one beneficiary and there is a Designated Beneficiary, the method for making distributions is outlined in Chapter 17.

If there's no Designated Beneficiary, the method for making distributions is outlined in Chapter 18.

CHAPTER 9

Required Minimum Distribution in the Year of the IRA Creator's Death

If the decedent didn't finish withdrawing the Required Minimum Distribution for the year of death, the beneficiary must do so

YOU MAY HAVE TO withdraw the Required Minimum Distribution for the year of the decedent's death by Dec. 31 of that year. If you should have made that withdrawal—but didn't—you'll have to pay a 50 percent penalty on the amount you should have withdrawn.[1] Sometimes, the IRS will waive the penalty.[2] (To learn about penalties and waivers, see Chapter 22.)

You are entitled to make the withdrawal because you, as the beneficiary, are entitled to all post-death IRA distributions, including

1 IRC § 4974. The decedent's estate and not the IRA beneficiary will owe the penalty if the decedent died after the last day for withdrawing a Required Minimum Distribution. For example, the decedent's estate will owe the penalty if the decedent died after April 1 of the year following the year when age 70 ½ was attained but failed to withdraw the Required Minimum Distribution with respect to the year when age 70 ½ was attained. For the year containing that April 1 due date, a second Required Minimum Distribution was due. If the decedent didn't withdraw that second Required Minimum Distribution, and if the beneficiary also fails to withdraw that amount by December 31 of that year, the beneficiary will owe the 50 percent penalty on that second distribution.

2 IRC § 4974(c) authorizes waiver of the 50 percent tax imposed under section 4974 if the taxpayer establishes to the satisfaction of the Secretary that (1) the shortfall described in section 4974(a) in the amount distributed during any taxable year was due to reasonable error, and (2) reasonable steps are being taken to remedy the shortfall.

the decedent's not-yet-withdrawn Required Minimum Distribution for the year of death.[3] The decedent's estate is not entitled to the decedent's Required Minimum Distribution if anyone besides the estate is the beneficiary of the decedent's IRA.

The withdrawal may be made either before or after the decedent's IRA is transferred (in a trustee-to-trustee transfer) to an Inherited IRA. But if you're the decedent's surviving spouse and you intend to roll over the decedent's IRA into your own IRA (instead of to an Inherited IRA), make sure you have withdrawn the Required Minimum Distribution before you make the rollover.

When Might You Have a Year-of-Death Withdrawal to Make?

You don't have a year-of-death withdrawal to make if the decedent died before reaching his Required Beginning Date[4]—even if death occurred one day before reaching the Required Beginning Date. (See Chapter 8 to ascertain the Required Beginning Date.)

On the other hand, if the decedent died on or after reaching his Required Beginning Date, you must check to see if the decedent had not withdrawn the Required Minimum Distribution for the year of death.

You only have a withdrawal obligation if the IRA creator should have taken a Required Minimum Distribution in the year of death, but didn't do so. Many IRAs are set up for automatic withdrawals, as frequently as monthly. The sum of the year's withdrawals might equal (or be slightly more than) the year's Required Minimum Distribution. However, when an IRA creator dies, those withdraw-

---

3 3 If the identity of the beneficiary (or beneficiaries) legally entitled to make withdrawals isn't clear, that could constitute grounds for obtaining waiver of the 50 percent tax imposed under section 4974.

4 4 IRC § 401(a)(9)(A) provides that distributions must be made on or after the Required Beginning Date. There is no requirement that Required Minimum Distributions commence prior to that date. Regs. § 1. 401(a)(9)-2, Q&A-2 similarly provides that, in order to satisfy required minim distributions, the either IRA creator's entire IRA must be distributed or distributions based on life expectancies must begin "not later than the Required Beginning Date". Regs. § 1.401(a)(9)-2, Q&A-4 specifically poses the question, "Must distributions made before the employee's required beginning date satisfy section 401(a)(9)?" The answer to that question provides that Required Minimum Distributions need not begin before the Required Begging Date, except when distributions in the form of periodic payments, such an annuity, actually begin before that date.

als probably stop. That would leave a shortfall in the year's Required Minimum Distribution, which you therefore must withdraw by year's end.

But not all IRAs are set up for automatic withdrawals. In that case, it's possible that you must withdraw all of the Required Minimum Distribution for the year of death.

How Much Must Be Withdrawn?

It's likely one of the decedent's advisors knows the amount that should have been withdrawn for the entire year. You will want to confirm that this amount is correct by making your own calculation.

There are three steps to take to determine how much, if any, you must withdraw.

Step 1: Determine the Decedent's Applicable Distribution Period

That's the number in the life expectancy table next to the age the decedent attained (or would have) attained in the year of death and/or the year when age 70½ was attained. The life expectancy table used by most IRA creators is the Uniform Table[5] (see Appendix C). There are two situations, however, in which the Uniform Table isn't used.

Situation 1: The decedent was married to a younger spouse. If the decedent was married on the first day of the year of death and the year of the spouse's birth was more than 10 years later than the year of the decedent's birth, the Joint and Survivor Table may be used.[6] For example, if the decedent was born in 1937 and the decedent's spouse was born in 1948 or later, use the Joint and Survivor Table.

Situation 2: The IRA was inherited by the decedent. If the decedent inherited the IRA and it was still an Inherited IRA at the time of the decedent's death, use the Single Life Table[7] (see Appendix D):

- If the decedent was the spouse of the person the decedent inherited the IRA from AND it was still an Inherited IRA at the time of the decedent's death AND the decedent also was the sole beneficiary of the Inherited IRA, look up the life

---

5 Regs. § § 1.401(a)(9)-5, Q&A-4(a) and 1.401(a)(9)-9, Q&A-2.

6 Regs. § § 1.401(a)(9)-5, Q&A-4(b) and 1.401(a)(9)-9, Q&A-3.

7 Regs. § § 1.401(a)(9)-5, Q&A-5(c)(1) and 1.401(a)(9)-9, Q&A-1

expectancy next to the age the decedent attained (or would have attained) in the year of death.[8] Thereafter, reduce by one each year.

- In all other cases in which the decedent inherited the Inherited IRA, look up the life expectancy next to the age the decedent attained (or would have) attained in the year after the year when the original IRA creator died; then reduce that number by one for each year thereafter up to the year when the decedent died.[9]

Step 2: Divide the IRA Value by the Decedent's Applicable Distribution Period

This step gives you the Required Minimum Distribution for the year of death. Use the value as of the beginning of the year when the IRA creator died.[10]

Step 3: Subtract the Year's Actual Withdrawals From the Year's Required Minimum Distribution

If you get a positive number, that's the amount to withdraw. If you get a negative number or zero, the Required Minimum Distribution was made and you aren't required to withdraw any more for that year. (You may not use the negative number to reduce the Required Minimum Distribution for the next year or for any other year.[11])

Decedent Owned More Than One IRA

If the decedent had several IRAs, IRS regulations say that the Required Minimum Distribution for each IRA must be determined separately.[12] But the Required Minimum Distribution of one account may be withdrawn from another, as long as the accounts are of the same "group". [13] The decedent's own IRAs are one group; IRAs the decedent inherited from the decedent's mother are a separate group;

---

8 See further, Chapter 20.
9 See further, Chapter 19.
10 Regs. § 1.401(a)(9)-5, Q&A-1(a).
11 Regs. § 1.401(a)(9)-5, Q&A-2.
12 Regs. § 1.408-8, Q&A-9, first sentence.
13 Regs. § 1.408-8, Q&A-9, Second sentence.

IRAs the decedent inherited from the decedent's father are a separate group, etc.[14]

What If You Tried and Failed?

Making a withdrawal before the end of the year may be a difficult, if not impossible, task, especially if the decedent dies late in the year. There will be paperwork you have to submit to establish you're the beneficiary and qualified to make the withdrawal. IRA trustees and custodians don't exactly move at the speed of light (or even at the speed of the Internet–and I recommend NOT using the Internet for any IRA transactions). Sometimes, individuals who work at the financial institution that holds the IRA aren't properly trained in the hundreds of forms they must use to deal with all of the investment and tax requirements that face them, so you'll have to be patient, self-informed and persistent.

If you did all you could, but still failed to get the withdrawal out of the IRA on time, you may very likely get a waiver of the 50 percent penalty tax from the IRS.[15] Just be sure you get the withdrawal out as soon as possible. To request the IRS waiver, you'll have to file IRS Form 5329, Additional Taxes on Qualified Plans (including IRAs) and Other Tax-Favored Accounts. Form 5329 must be filed with your individual income tax return.[16] Report the 50 percent tax on Form 5329, and attach your request for penalty waiver. The request should indicate why you believe you're entitled to the waiver, and show that you have taken out the missed withdrawal.[17] (For additional details, see Chapter 22.)

---

14 Regs. § 1.408-8, Q&A-9.

15 IRC § 4974(d).

16 In your author's experience, if an individual income tax return was filed (or was required to be filed) for the year when the failure to distribute any part or all of a Required Minimum Distribution occurred, the IRS will reject Form 5329 if it's not attached to an amended or original income tax return. This is so, even though Form 5329 has it's own signature block.

17 See instructions to Form 5329.

CHAPTER 10

Who's a "Designated Beneficiary"?

An "IRA beneficiary" isn't the same as a "Designated Beneficiary"

A CRITICAL TASK IN complying with Required Minimum Distributions is figuring out whether there's a "Designated Beneficiary."

This chapter applies to the beneficiaries of an IRA created by the decedent. (If you have inherited an IRA that the decedent inherited from another original IRA creator, see Part 4 of this book instead).

In Part 3 of this book, there's a separate chapter for each of the most common beneficiary designations. But before you turn there, you'll need to read this chapter so you'll know what's meant by the term "Designated Beneficiary." This chapter also discusses actions that can be taken to improve things after the IRA creator dies.

IRA beneficiaries are entitled to receive IRA distributions of the cash or investments held inside the IRA.[1] The IRA benefi-

1 The identity of IRA death beneficiaries may be determined by inspecting documents that establish the IRA and govern its operation. Typically, there is either an IRA trust agreement (for trusteed IRAs) or an IRA adoption agreement (for custodial IRAs). An IRA beneficiary form can be part of the trust or adoption agreement, or it can be a separate document. Inspect these documents, even if a notice has been received from the IRA trustee or custodian stating who the IRA beneficiary is. State law may also establish entitlement to benefits. Rights to IRA benefits can change when an IRA beneficiary makes a disclaimer (a refusal to accept IRA benefits in accordance with applicable state law). Other examples of state law application to IRA benefits include community property rights or marital dissolution rights.

ciaries are fixed as of the date of the IRA creator's death.[2] Required Minimum Distributions must usually be withdrawn by each and every IRA beneficiary over the life expectancy of one (and only one) IRA beneficiary, provided there's a beneficiary who fits the definition of "Designated Beneficiary."[3] There may be no Designated Beneficiary even though the IRA has one or more beneficiaries.

When it comes to Required Minimum Distributions, there may be many IRA beneficiaries, but there can only ever be one "Designated Beneficiary."

"Designated Beneficiary" is a term that has meaning only in the context of Required Minimum Distributions. The Designated Beneficiary is the person whose age controls the number of years over which Required Minimum Distributions are made.[4] The identity of the Designated Beneficiary, if one exists, is fixed as of Sept. 30 of the year after the year when the IRA creator died,[5] to allow time for taking post-death actions that can change for the better whom the Designated Beneficiary is, or even to eliminate any IRA beneficiary who can't qualify as a Designated Beneficiary.

You are the Designated Beneficiary if you meet all three of the following criteria:[6]

1. You are an individual,

2. You are named as the IRA's only death beneficiary, and

3. You have the right to receive all distributions made from the IRA during your lifetime.

If you are the Designated Beneficiary because you meet all three criteria, you don't need to read the rest of this chapter.

If you don't meet all three of those criteria, read on.

---

2 Rights to IRA benefits can change when an IRA beneficiary makes a disclaimer (a refusal to accept IRA benefits in accordance with applicable state law). See Chapter 26.
3 IRC § 401(a)(9)(B); Regs. § 1.401(a)(9)-5 Q&A-5(c)(3).
4 Regs. § 1.401(a)(9)-4.
5 Regs. § 1.401(a)(9)-5 Q&A-5(a). If the decedent died on or after reaching the Required Beginning Date, and if the number of years that would have been the decedent's remaining life expectancy is greater than the Designated Beneficiary's life expectancy, then the decedent's remaining life expectancy is used instead of the Designated Beneficiary's life expectancy.
6 Regs. § 1.401(a)(9)-5 Q&A-5, Q&A-7.

Here's some bad news: The IRA beneficiary with the shortest life expectancy (in other words, the oldest one) is the Designated Beneficiary. [7]

Here's some worse news: If any IRA beneficiary isn't an individual or a "see-through trust" (more on trusts, later), there's no Designated Beneficiary,[8] even though the list of IRA beneficiaries includes one or more individuals. If there's no Designated Beneficiary, and the IRA creator died before reaching the Required Beginning Date, the entire IRA will typically have to be withdrawn (in taxable distributions) by Dec. 31 of the fifth year after the year of the IRA creator's death.[9] A common example leading to this result is when an estate is the IRA beneficiary (remember: even if the IRA creator made a will, there still won't be a Designated Beneficiary). Another common example is when a charity is one of the IRA beneficiaries (or the only IRA beneficiary).

Here's some better news: In many cases, problems can be fixed, and things can be improved. But you have to know the rules to take advantage of those opportunities.

Divide and Conquer: Turn One IRA With Many Beneficiaries Into Several IRAs With Only One Beneficiary Each

It's a lot of trouble for several beneficiaries to "share" one IRA. Most would rather have the control over the Inherited IRA that comes with being the only beneficiary. And, if, for instance, you're 45 years old, you don't want to have to take distributions over the relatively shorter life expectancy of your aunt, who is 68 years old.

You can carve out your own Inherited IRA and that will give you full control over your share, and possibly the right to use your own life expectancy for Required Minimum Distributions as well (no matter who else is also a beneficiary of the decedent's IRA).[10] But there's a deadline: to be able to use your own life expectancy, you must transfer your share of the decedent's IRA into your own Inherited IRA by

---

7 Regs. § 1.401(a)(9)-5 Q&A-7(a)(1).
8 Regs. § 1.401(a)(9)-4, Q&A-3.
9 IRC § 401(a)(9)(B); Regs. § 1.401(a)(9)-5(c)(3).
10 Regs. § 1.401(a)(9)-8, Q&A-2.

Dec. 31 of the year after the IRA creator's death (it's best to do it much earlier).[11] The details are in Chapter 11.

To make a transfer to your own Inherited IRA and be treated as its Designated Beneficiary, you must be an *actual* beneficiary of the decedent's IRA named on the IRA's beneficiary designation form.[12] You can't be treated as the only Designated Beneficiary if you received your part of the decedent's IRA because you're a beneficiary of the decedent's estate that became entitled to the IRA, or because you're one of several beneficiaries of a trust that was the IRA's beneficiary.

How to Identify the Designated Beneficiary

When there's more than one beneficiary, it takes four steps to identify the Designated Beneficiary:

> *Step 1:* List all possible recipients of IRA distributions whose right to future distributions exist as of the decedent's date of death. These are the Designated Beneficiary candidates.

> *Step 2:* Cross off the list of Designated Beneficiary candidates any candidate who's a mere successor beneficiary.

> *Step 3:* Cross off the list of Designated Beneficiary candidates any who are no longer Designated Beneficiary candidates by Sept. 30 of the year after the decedent's date of death. The list that remains is the final Designated Beneficiary candidates list.

> *Step 4:* Identify the Designated Beneficiary from the final Designated Beneficiary candidates list. The Designated Beneficiary is the oldest member of the Designated Beneficiary candidates list.

Now, let's look at each of these four steps in more detail.

Step 1: List all possible recipients of IRA distributions.

The first step in finding out who, if anyone, is a Designated Beneficiary, is to make a list of all possible beneficiaries. This list is made as of the IRA creator's date of death.[13] The candidates list includes any person

---

11 Regs. § 1.401(a)(9)-8, Q&A-2(a)(2).

12 Only a person who is legally actually entitled to death benefits of an IRA has the legal ability to cause that persons portion of an account to be transferred to an IRA held for that person's benefit alone.

13 Regs. § 1.401(a)(9)-4, Q&A-4(a).

who is possibly entitled to a distribution, ever.[14] The resulting list is the list of Designated Beneficiary candidates.

Making this list can be tricky. "Possible" doesn't mean "likely" —you can't exclude a possible recipient of IRA distributions from the list just because there's only a remote chance that person will actually ever get any part of the IRA.[15]

> EXAMPLE: Jared is Jolene's son. Jolene established a trust and named Jared as beneficiary. The trust was named beneficiary of Jolene's IRA. Jared was 20 years old when Jolene died. The trust pays Jared income until he reaches age 30. When Jared reaches age 30, the trust will give all of its assets to Jared, including all of the trust's rights in Jolene's IRA. But if Jared dies before reaching age 30, the trust will give all of its assets to Renee, Jared's aunt. Renee attained age 67 the year Jolene died. Renee cannot be eliminated from the list of possible Designated Beneficiaries just because it isn't likely Jared will die before reaching age 30.

Step 2: Cross off the list of Designated Beneficiary candidates any candidate who's a mere successor beneficiary.

A mere successor beneficiary is a candidate who can only receive IRA distribution proceeds because another beneficiary has died, who, while

---

14 Regs. § 1.401(a)(9)-4, Q&A-1 provides that the Designated Beneficiary must attain such status under the plan. The beneficiary must be a beneficiary either under the terms of the plan itself or, if the plan so provides, must be designated to the plan by an affirmative action taken by the participant. Rights conferred under other means, such as by reason of application of state law, will not make an individual so entitled a required minimum distributions Designated Beneficiary unless the beneficiary is also named under the plan. Beneficiaries need not be specified by name, and may be designated by naming a class capable of expansion or contraction. An example would be children of the participant, by right of representation (in some states, per stirpes). But in all cases, the beneficiary must be identifiable under the terms of the plan both as of the date for determining the Designated Beneficiary and as of the date of the participant's death.

15 See, for example, PLR 200228025. The example appearing after the Footnote 15 reference is based on that PLR.

living, is entitled to all distributions from the IRA following the death of the IRA creator.[16]

> EXAMPLE: In the Jared example, above, if Jolene's trust for Jared had said that Jared was entitled to receive the proceeds of all IRA distributions paid to the trust until Jared reaches age 30, when the trust will give the IRA to Jared, then Renee would be eliminated as a possible Designated Beneficiary.

Before we go on to Step 3, let's look at some common situations to get a better feel for how to make the date-of-death list.

Scenario 1: One Primary Beneficiary

If an IRA creator is married, the IRA beneficiary form will sometimes list the IRA creator's spouse as the only primary beneficiary. This primary beneficiary designation is often accompanied by naming children as "contingent" or "alternate" beneficiaries, in case the spouse dies before the IRA creator does. If the IRA creator dies and the IRA creator's spouse survives the decedent, the surviving spouse is the only person to list as a candidate, and will, as the only candidate, become the Designated Beneficiary. But if the IRA creator's spouse dies before the IRA creator, the children will all become Designated Beneficiary candidates.

Scenario 2: Two Primary Beneficiaries

What if there are two primary beneficiaries, and one of them has died before the IRA creator did? Read the beneficiary form carefully to see what happens to that deceased beneficiary's share. Here's where the labels on IRA beneficiary forms can be misleading. Sometimes the IRA beneficiary form has fine print that says the share of a primary beneficiary who dies before the IRA creator goes to the other primary beneficiary and not to the persons listed under the part of the form called "contingent" or "alternate" beneficiaries. In those beneficiary forms, all primary beneficiaries must die before the IRA creator does, for a "contingent" or "alternate" beneficiary to get one cent. Other times, the share goes to one or more of the contingent or alternate beneficiaries and not to the surviving primary beneficiary. Even so,

---

16 Regs. § 1.401(a)(9)-5, Q&A-7(c)

it's possible to fill out the name of the primary beneficiary in a way that achieves a different result. For example, if there's some language written after the beneficiary's name (for example, "per stirpes" or "by right of representation"), check with a qualified attorney to interpret the beneficiary form and to find out what any "extra" language might mean.

Scenario 3: Trust as Beneficiary

If a trust was named as an IRA's beneficiary, and if that trust qualifies as a "see-through" trust, then all possible beneficiaries of that trust are Designated Beneficiary candidates and must be considered in determining who (if anyone) is the Designated Beneficiary.[17] Also, when there's a see-through trust, the trust itself is crossed off the Designated Beneficiary candidates list.[18]

To be a "see-through" trust, a trust must pass all four of these tests:

1. The trust must be irrevocable (meaning not able to be changed) no later than the time when the IRA creator dies. It can be irrevocable at an earlier time, but not at a later time;

2. The trust must be a valid trust under state law (but ignore whether having nothing owned by the trust could make the trust fail to be valid);

3. The trust's beneficiaries must be identifiable from the trust document; and

4. A copy of the trust (or a certified list of beneficiaries) must be given to the IRA custodian by Oct. 31 of the year after the IRA creator's death.[19]

If a trust is not a see-through trust, then there is no Designated Beneficiary.

Trusts are usually complicated to read, requiring the services of someone who has experience with trusts to help make the Designated Beneficiary candidates list.

---

17 Regs. § 1.401(a)(9)-4, Q&A-5&6.

18 That's because see-through status depends solely on the identity of the trust's beneficiaries.

19 Regs. § 1.401(a)(9)-4, Q&A-5. Requirements for providing a copy of the trust or a certified list of its beneficiaries to the IRA trustee or custodian are provided in Regs. § 1.401(a)(9)-4, Q&A-6.

Step 3: Can Anyone Be Crossed Off the List?

Any Designated Beneficiary candidate who dies after the IRA creator but before Sept. 30 of the year following the year of the IRA creator's death must stay on the list[20]—a helpful rule that tends to assure that someone's life expectancy may be used for making annual Required Minimum Distributions.

Designated Beneficiary candidates can be eliminated from the date-of-death list in three situations. It's best to have an estate planning attorney help with this because beneficiary forms are legal documents that can be difficult to interpret.

Situation 1: Cross off any beneficiary who gets nothing until after another beneficiary who has the right to receive all distributions for life dies.[21]

Read the IRA beneficiary form to see who can be crossed of the list for this reason. There's usually a section on the forms for "primary" beneficiaries like Philida, and another section for "contingent" or "secondary" beneficiaries like Rachel. In most cases, the "contingent" or "secondary" beneficiaries" can be crossed off the list.

For example, Philida and Rachel are both named as beneficiaries, but Philida is entitled to all IRA distributions as long as she's alive. Rachel is not a Designated Beneficiary candidate.

Situation 2: Cross off anyone who gets "cashed out" by Sept. 30 of the year after the year when IRA creator died.[22]

This is one way that Required Minimum Distributions can be lowered, and IRS regulations specifically say so. For example, say that the IRA creator's child is named as beneficiary of 50 percent of the IRA. A charity is named as the other 50 percent beneficiary. If half of the IRA is distributed to the charity by Sept. 30 of the year after the year when IRA creator died, the charity is crossed off of the list of Designated Beneficiary candidates. The child then becomes the only IRA beneficiary left by Sept. 30 and therefore becomes the Designated Beneficiary.

Situation 3: Cross off anyone who disclaims all of his or her

---

20 Regs. § 1.401(a)(9)-4, Q&A-4(c).

21 Regs. § 1.401(a)(9)-5, Q&A-7(c).

22 Regs. § 1.401(a)(9)-4, Q&A-4(a).

share of the decedent's IRA by Sept. 30 of the year after the IRA creator's death.

This is another way that Required Minimum Distributions can be lowered, and IRS regulations specifically say so.[23] No person has to accept a gift or an inheritance. A "disclaimer" is the legal name for a written refusal to accept a gift or an inheritance.[24] The disclaimer must be made within nine months of the IRA creator's date of death or, if the person who wishes to disclaim is under age 21, it must be made by Sept. 30 of the year after the IRA creator's death (if applicable state laws say the beneficiary isn't old enough to disclaim, someone who is old enough to act on that person's behalf will have to be appointed to make the disclaimer).[25] Sept. 30 of the year after the year when IRA creator died is the latest a disclaimer can be made if the person making the disclaimer is to be crossed of the Designated Beneficiary candidates list.[26] There's more on disclaimers in Chapter 26.

Step 4: Identify the Designated Beneficiary

On Sept. 30 of the year after the IRA creator's death, the Designated Beneficiary candidates list is final, and the Designated Beneficiary can be identified (if there is one).

Using the Designated Beneficiary candidates list that remains after Step 3, determine whether all Designated Beneficiary candidates are individuals. If even one Designated Beneficiary candidate that remains after Step 3 isn't an individual, there's no Designated Beneficiary. [27]

But if all candidates are individuals, the one with the shortest life expectancy (meaning the oldest one) is the Designated Beneficiary.[28]

It's possible to avoid the rule that the eldest of several beneficiaries will become the Designated Beneficiary. The rule can be avoided if each beneficiary has a separate Inherited IRA that holds his or her share of the decedent's IRA. The separate IRAs must be established

---

23 Regs. § 1.401(a)(9)-4, Q&A-4(a).

24 Disclaimers should comply with applicable state law.

25 IRC § 2518 provides that a "qualified" disclaimer will not be regarded as a taxable gift made by the disclaimant. A discussion of those requirements is beyond the scope of this work.

26 Regs. § 1.401(a)(9)-4, Q&A-4(a), last sentence.

27 Regs. § 1.401(a)(9)-4, Q&A-2&3; Regs. § 1.401(a)(9)-5, Q&A-7(a).

28 Regs. § 1.401(a)(9)-5, Q&A-7(a)(1).

by Dec. 31, of the year following the year of the decedent's death. See Chapter 11 for details regarding separate accounts.

Here are some examples of identifying the Designated Beneficiary:

- There's only one beneficiary. That one beneficiary is the Designated Beneficiary.

- There are several beneficiaries who are all individuals; they're the decedent's surviving spouse and children. The oldest among them is the Designated Beneficiary (it might not be the surviving spouse if the decedent had children by a previous marriage).

- There are three equal IRA death beneficiaries who are all individuals. By Dec. 31 of the year after the year when the IRA creator died, the IRA is divided into one Inherited IRA per beneficiary. Each IRA death beneficiary is the Designated Beneficiary of his or her own Inherited IRA.

- For 80 percent of an IRA, several beneficiaries who are all individuals are beneficiaries. A charity is the beneficiary of the other 20 percent of the IRA. There's no Designated Beneficiary, because the charity isn't an individual. But, if there's an IRA distribution to the charity of the charity's entire 20 percent share of the IRA by Sept. 30 of the year after the year when the IRA creator died, the eldest of the individuals will be the Designated Beneficiary. The individuals may be able to divide up the IRA so that each can use his own life expectancy for Required Minimum Distributions.

- The IRA beneficiary is an estate. There's no Designated Beneficiary because the estate isn't an individual. But, if the surviving spouse is entitled to the IRA as beneficiary of the estate, the surviving spouse might be able to make a rollover of the IRA to an IRA of her own. For more, see Chapter 25.

CHAPTER 11

Creating Separate Accounts

Here's how two or more beneficiaries can create separate accounts

WHEN AN IRA CREATOR dies, leaving a decedent's IRA, creating one Inherited IRA for each of the IRA's death beneficiaries can make it possible for each beneficiary to be the Designated Beneficiary of his or her own separate Inherited IRA. Each separate Inherited IRA must be established and funded no later than Dec. 31 of the year after the year when the IRA creator died[1]–please don't wait until the last minute.

Each beneficiary who wants to establish a separate Inherited IRA must be entitled to a portion of the decedent's IRA. A beneficiary is entitled to a portion of a decedent's IRA if the beneficiary form says a fraction (one third, for example) or a percentage of the account is payable to that beneficiary. Each separate Inherited IRA must be established for only one of the beneficiaries named in the IRA's beneficiary form. Each separate Inherited IRA must hold each beneficiary's respective share of the decedent's IRA.

> EXAMPLE: Each of four beneficiaries is entitled to 25 percent of a decedent's IRA. Each beneficiary establishes an Inherited IRA by Dec. 31 of the year after the year when the IRA creator died. By that Dec. 31, each 25 percent share of the decedent's IRA is trans-

1 Reg. § 1.401(a)(9)-8, Q&A- A-2(a)(2). This portion of the regulations is the basis for all of this Chapter 11.

ferred directly from the decedent's IRA to each of the four Inherited IRAs in a in a so-called trustee-to-trustee transfer.

Once a separate Inherited IRA is established in accordance with the all of the rules, it's as though the beneficiary of that separate Inherited IRA received that Inherited IRA from the decedent as of the date of the decedent's death. For any beneficiary with a separate Inherited IRA, that beneficiary will be the Designated Beneficiary for purposes of making Required Minimum Distributions (see Chapter 11). For a surviving spouse, that means Required Minimum Distributions from the separate account may begin on the spouse's Required Commencement Date (see Chapter 14). Each beneficiary who may avoid the five-year rule (see Chapter 8) by electing to take Required Minimum Distributions beginning by Dec. 31 of the year following the IRA creator's year of death is in control of that election without regard to what other beneficiaries of the other separate Inherited IRAs decide.

CHAPTER 12

Surviving Spouses Only: Make It Your Own IRA

Making a spousal rollover or direct transfer transforms the IRA creator's IRA into your own IRA, just as though you created the IRA in the first place.

MAKING YOUR DECEASED SPOUSE'S IRA your own may lower your lifetime annual Required Minimum Distributions from a traditional IRA and eliminate all lifetime Required Minimum Distributions from a Roth IRA. To figure out if that will lower your Required Minimum Distributions, see Chapters 14 and 15. Once you make an IRA your own, you become the IRA creator.

What Can You Make Your Own?

If the IRA creator left you a traditional IRA, you may transfer or rollover from the decedent's traditional IRA to a traditional IRA held in your own name.[1]

If the IRA creator left you a Roth IRA, you may make a transfer or rollover from the decedent's Roth IRA to a Roth IRA held in your name.[2]

---

1 IRC § 408(d)(6).

2 IRC § 408A generally subjects Roth IRAs to the traditional IRA rules of § 408, including § 408(d)(6) spousal rollover rules. Roth IRAs differ from traditional IRAs only as provided in § 408A. Specifically, § 408A(a) provides that "a Roth IRA shall be treated for purposes of [the Internal Revenue Code] in the same manner as an individual retirement plan." § 7701(a)(37) defines "individual retirement plan" to mean "(A) an individual retirement

You may also convert a traditional IRA of the IRA creator to a Roth IRA of your own by making a rollover or a direct transfer to a Roth IRA held in your name, a decision you should evaluate carefully, as you'll have to pay income taxes on the Roth IRA conversion.[3]

What Effect Will Making the IRA Your Own Have if You're Under Age 59½?

If you're under age 59½ there may be a downside to making the decedent's IRA your own: the 10 percent tax on IRA withdrawals before age 59½ can apply.[4]   (See Chapter 21 for exceptions.)

It doesn't have to be all or none. You could determine, as part of your overall financial plan, that some amount you won't need before reaching age 59½ can be converted to your own IRA, while the amount you might need before then can be transferred to an Inherited IRA. After reaching age 59½, when the 10 percent tax no longer applies, any amount remaining in the Inherited IRA can be converted to your own IRA. If you do transfer some part to an Inherited IRA, you must follow the Inherited IRA rules when it comes to making Required Minimum Distributions from that Inherited IRA. (See Chapter 14.)

A Required Minimum Distribution may not be rolled over.[5] Be sure to withdraw the decedent's final Required Minimum Distribution, to the extent the decedent didn't withdraw it. Also, don't transfer or roll over your own Required Minimum Distribution. Withdraw these amounts first, then make the decedent's IRA your own. If you don't,

---

account described in section 408(a), and (B) an individual retirement annuity described in section 408(b)".

3 A surviving spouse may convert a deceased spouse's traditional IRA to a Roth IRA by taking these steps in order. First, make the election to treat the decedent's traditional IRA as an IRA of the surviving spouse (see later in this chapter). Second, once that election has been made, the IRA, now a traditional IRA of the surviving spouse, can be converted to a Roth IRA. Another, simpler method of converting a deceased spouse's traditional IRA to a Roth IRA of the surviving spouse is for the surviving spouse to make either a direct transfer (preferred) or a rollover from the decedent's traditional IRA to a Roth IRA of the surviving spouse. By so doing, the surviving spouse has elected to treat the decedent's IRA as an IRA of the surviving spouse because the surviving spouse has "[redesignated] the [decedent's] account as an account in the name of the surviving spouse as IRA owner rather than as beneficiary."

4 IRC § 72(t).

5 Reg. § 1.408-8, Q&A-4. But, see Q&A-5, which can have the effect of reducing Required Minimum Distribution by reason of electing to treat a decedent's IRA as an IRA of the surviving spouse.

the transfer or rollover will include Required Minimum Distributions not yet withdrawn, causing an excess IRA contribution subject to penalties.[6]

Open a New IRA In Your Own Name

Your first step in making an IRA your own is to open an IRA account in your own name.

Be sure to name beneficiaries for your Rollover IRA. As naming beneficiaries is part of your estate plan, consult with your estate planning team. Once your Rollover IRA is in place, you can change beneficiaries as often as you wish. For example, should you marry again, any or all of your spousal rollover IRA can be left to your new spouse, who may also make a rollover after your death.

Two Ways to Make It Your Own IRA

Once you have opened your Rollover IRA, there are two ways to make a spousal rollover: direct transfer or spousal rollover.

The best route is a direct transfer from the IRA creator's IRA to your new IRA. That's because, when it comes to rollovers, there are two tripping points. First, there's a 60-day deadline for completing the deposit to your new IRA, and it's all too easy for 60 days to slip by without completing that deposit.[7] Second, only one rollover is allowed in any twelve-month period.[8]

The rollover method will be needed if you receive a distribution from the IRA creator's IRA, meaning a check was made out in your name or there was a distribution deposited directly into a non-IRA account you own. There are other ways that a surviving spouse can elect to treat a decedent's IRA as an IRA of the surviving spouse. These other ways have problems. It can take some detection work to determine whether such an election has been made. Also, an election can be made without even knowing that has occurred.

---

6 IRC § 4973 imposes a tax at the rate of 15 percent on excess contributions to an IRA. Excess contributions are amounts contributed to an IRA in excess of deductible contributions. Certain exceptions apply. For example, the tax does not apply to rollover contributions.

7 IRC § 408(d)(3)(A).

8 IRC § 408(d)(3)(B).

The other ways to elect to treat your deceased spouse's IRA as your own are:

- You failed to make Required Minimum Distributions as required of a beneficiary; [9]
- You have withdrawn Required Minimum Distributions in the same way you would if you had made a rollover, and that amount is less than Required Minimum Distributions required of you as beneficiary; [10]
- You made a contribution to the IRA (requires examining the IRA for contributions by the surviving spouse).[11] This method of electing to treat a deceased spouse's IRA as an IRA of the surviving spouse seems unlikely because the financial institutions that offer IRAs generally won't permit a surviving spouse to make a contribution to an IRA of a deceased spouse; or,
- You retitle the IRA in your own name. This method of electing to treat a deceased spouse's IRA as an IRA of the surviving spouse seems unlikely because the financial institutions that offer IRAs generally won't permit a title change. But the preferred method of making a direct transfer from the decedent's IRA to an IRA you set up in your own name is essentially the same thing as retitling the account in your own name. [12]

Bottom line: The most reliable and straightforward path is a direct transfer.

How is a Direct Transfer Accomplished?

To make a direct transfer of some or all of the decedent's IRA, direct the IRA trustee of the decedent's IRA to transfer cash or investments

9 Regs. § 1.408-8, Q&A-5(b). Although this regulation provides that the election may not be made where a trust is beneficiary of the decedent's account, the IRS has, in numerous private letter rulings, permitted to the spouse to make a rollover where the spouse actually receives the proceeds of the decedent's account. See, for example, private letter ruling 201507040 (12/24/2014), where a decedent's IRA was payable to a trust and spouse, in her capacity as trustee of that took affirmative action authorized under the terms of the trust, thereby causing distribution of IRA proceeds to herself in her individual capacity. Held: surviving spouse may make a rollover of IRA proceeds actually received by her.

10 Regs. § 1.408-8, Q&A-5(b).

11 Ibid, note 8.

12 Ibid, note 8.

from the decedent's IRA directly to your new IRA. There should be no check made out to you. Many IRA withdrawal forms include the direct transfer option (see Chapter 5.(

How Will a Making the IRA Your Own Affect Beneficiaries You Name for Your New IRA?

Once you make the decedent's IRA your own, beneficiaries you name for your rollover IRA will be able to use their own life expectancies for Required Minimum Distributions after your death (see Chaper 16.)

CHAPTER 13

Who's a "Surviving Spouse"? The Answer Changed During 2013

For all Federal tax purposes, the definition of marriage now includes any same-sex marriage entered into in a state where that's permitted. Some surviving spouses may be able to fix problems

The U. S. Supreme Court Decided Same Sex Marriages Must Be Recognized by Federal Laws

ON JUNE 26, 2013, the United States Supreme Court held that federal laws must recognize marriages of same-sex couples validly entered into, provided the couple resides in a state that recognizes the marriage. The formal name of that landmark case is: UNITED STATES, PETITIONER V. EDITH SCHLAIN WINDSOR, IN HER CAPACITY AS EXECUTOR OF THE ESTATE OF THEA CLARA SPYER, ET AL.[1]

States Must Recognize Same-Sex Marriages

On June 26, 2015, the United States Supreme Court held that, because the United States Constitution's fourteenth amendment guarantees all U.S. citizens equal protection under the law, all states must license same-sex marriages and also must recognize same-sex marriages validly entered into in another state or foreign country.[2]

1 133 S. Ct. 2675 (2013).
2 Obergefell et al. V. Hodges, Director, Ohio Department Of Health, et al., No. 14–556, U.S. (2015)

The Fourteenth Amendment requires a State to license a marriage between two people of the same sex and to recognize a marriage between two people of the same sex when their marriage was lawfully licensed and performed out-of-State.

The formal name of that landmark case is: OBERGEFELL ET AL. v. HODGES, DIRECTOR, OHIO DEPARTMENT OF HEALTH, ET AL

Effect of Supreme Court Decision on Tax Laws and Retirement Accounts

In response to the *Windsor* decision, on August 29, 2013, the United States Treasury and the Internal Revenue Service announced that they would do likewise when applying all federal tax laws, except that it doesn't matter whether the state where the couple lives recognizes the marriage.[3] It only matters that the marriage was entered into in a state or country that authorized the marriage.

"Marriage" includes a common law marriage, defined as a union of two people created by agreement followed by cohabitation that is legally recognized by a state. According to Treasury and IRS, common-law marriages have three basic features: (1) A present agreement to be married, (2) cohabitation, and (3) public representations of marriage.[4]

"Marriage" does not include, as far as Treasury and IRS are concerned, any registered domestic partnership, civil union, or other similar formal relationship recognized under state law that is not denominated as a marriage under the laws of that state.[5]

---

3 Rev. Rul. 2013-17; 2013-38 I.R.B. 201; Amplified by Notice 2014-19; Amplified by Notice 2014-1; Amplifies and Clarifies Rev. Rul. 58-66. The Internal Revenue Service recognized all same-sex marriages entered into under valid state law. Under the U.S. Supreme Court's decision in Obegerfell, all states must license same-sex marriages. Presumably, that should mean all states must recognize pre-Obegerfell marriages entered into in any state that licensed same-sex marriages.

4 Ibid, note 2.

5 Ibid, note 2.

Is Retroactive Relief Available?

As of this book's date of publication, the IRS has not yet announced what actions may be taken retroactively when it comes to inheriting an IRA.

This much is obvious: Any amounts now standing in an Inherited IRA that could have been rolled over to an IRA of the surviving spouse may now be rolled over. For any amounts not rolled over that remain in an Inherited IRA:

- If the IRA creator died before reaching his/her Required Beginning Date, determine your Required Commencement Date (see Chapter 14). If your Required Commencement Date hasn't occurred yet, you may stop taking Required Minimum Distributions until that date.

- Determine your Applicable Distribution Period as a surviving spouse (see Chapter 14).

Beyond the obvious, the IRS may announce other kinds of relief. For example:

- If your marriage had been recognized at the time of the IRA creator's death, a rollover to your IRA would have been possible (see Chapters 12 and 15).

- It also would have been possible to elect to treat the IRA you inherited as an IRA of your own (see Chapter 15).

PART 3

REQUIRED MINIMUM DISTRIBUTIONS
—
YOU INHERITED AN IRA FROM THE IRA'S CREATOR

CHAPTER 14

Your Required Minimum Distributions: You're the IRA Creator's Surviving Spouse – Option 1, Spousal Inherited IRA

*Your Required Commencement Date depends on whether the IRA creator died before reaching **his/her** Required Beginning Date. After Required Minimum Distributions begin, look up your Applicable Distribution Period each year*

THIS CHAPTER APPLIES TO you if:

- You're the IRA creator's surviving spouse, and
- You do not elect to treat the IRA as an IRA of your own.

See the next chapter if you are electing to treat the IRA as an IRA of your own, including by making a rollover. Even if you do not elect to treat the IRA as an IRA of your own at this time, you may do so at any time, even years later.[1]

If the IRA Creator Died Before Reaching His/Her Required Beginning Date, Determine Your Required Commencement Date

If the IRA creator died before reaching his/her Required Beginning Date (see Chapter 8), and you are the sole beneficiary of the IRA cre-

---

1 See Chapter 15.

ator's account, your Required Commencement Date is the date when your first Required Minimum Distribution is due.[2] If you are one of several beneficiaries, you may be able to create an account that you are the sole beneficiary of. Creating a separate account is covered in Chapter 11.

Your Required Commencement Date is similar to an IRA creator's Required Beginning Date: it's the last date when you must take your first Required Minimum Distribution based on your life expectancy (unless the five-year rule applies).[3]

Your Required Commencement Date is Dec. 31 of the year the IRA creator would have reached age 70½ if the IRA creator had continued living.[4] But your Required Commencement Date is never earlier than Dec. 31 of the year *after* the year when the IRA creator died.[5]

> EXAMPLE: Alice, born July 7, 1941, died on January 20, 2010 at age 68. Her Required Beginning Date would have occurred on Apr. 1, 2013, if she had lived. Alice left her IRA to her husband, Teddy, who reached age 74 in the year of Alice's death. Teddy's Required Commencement Date is Dec. 31, 2012 because Alice would have reached age 70½ in that year (not Alice's Apr. 1, 2013 Required Beginning Date year). Teddy's age doesn't matter when it comes to an Inherited IRA's Required Commencement Date.
>
> But if Alice dies during 2012, Teddy's Required Commencement Date is Dec. 31, 2013 because Teddy's Required Commencement Date is never earlier than Dec. 31 of the year *after* the year when Alice died.
>
> And if Alice dies during 2013 but before Apr. 1 (her Required Beginning Date), Teddy's Required Commencement Date is Dec. 31, 2014.

---

2 IRC § 401(a)(9)(B)(iv); Regs. § 1.401(a)(9)-3, Q&A-3(b).

3 Ibid, note 2.

4 Ibid, note 2.

5 Ibid, note 2.

Can the Five-Year Rule Apply?

Making distributions in accordance with a surviving spouse's Required Commencement Date eliminates possible application of the five-year rule (covered in Chapter 8). An employer's qualified plan's governing documents can force application of the five-year rule, but transfer to an Inherited IRA of the surviving spouse by Dec. 31 of the year after the year of the decedent's death will defeat application of the five-year rule.

Figuring Your Required Minimum Distributions

If the five-year rule doesn't apply to your Inherited IRA, each year's Required Minimum Distribution is equal to the value of the IRA at the beginning of the year, divided by your "Applicable Distribution Period."[6]

Your Applicable Distribution Period is determined each year, as follows. For each year beginning with the year following the year when the decedent died, find the age you will be on Dec. 31 of that year in the Single Life Table (See Appendix D). The life expectancy number listed next to the age you will be on that Dec. 31 is your Applicable Distribution Period.[7]

In the first Alice and Teddy example, Teddy's Required Commencement Date is Dec. 31, 2012. Teddy is age 76 in 2012. His Applicable Distribution Period for 2012 from the Single Life Table is 12.7.

On Dec. 31, 2011, the value of Alice's IRA was $200,000. Teddy's 2012 Required Minimum Distribution is $15,748.03 ($200,000 divided by 12.7). Teddy must withdraw that amount by Dec. 31, 2012.

---

6 Regs. § 1.401(a)(9)-5, Q&A-1(a).
7 Regs. § 1.401(a)(9)-5, Q&A-5(c)(2).

Here are Teddy's Applicable Distribution Periods for several years:

Year	Age	Applicable Distribution Period
2012	76	12.7
2013	77	12.1
2014	78	11.4
2015	79	10.8
2016	80	10.2

The table shows Teddy's Applicable Distribution Period doesn't decrease by one each year. The table has Applicable Distribution Periods all the way out to age 111. So, Teddy's last Required Minimum Distribution won't occur until Teddy reaches age 111, should he live so long.

If Teddy wants to lower his Required Minimum Distributions, electing to treat the IRA as his own or making a rollover to his own IRA will accomplish that. Teddy can take advantage of either option at any time. When he does, he'll use the Uniform Table instead of the Single Life Table, beginning in the year of his election or rollover. For example, if Teddy makes the election in the year he turns age 77, his Applicable Distribution Period will be 21.2 instead of 12.1. Assuming the Dec. 31, 2012 value of the IRA was $190,000, his Required Minimum Distribution would be $8,962.26 ($190,000 divided by 21.2) rather than $15,702.48 ($190,000 divided by 12.1).

If the IRA Creator Died After Reaching His/Her Required Beginning Date

Each year, you must perform three steps to determine your Applicable Distribution Period:

Step 1:

Find the age you will be on Dec. 31 of the year after the year when the IRA creator died in the Single Life Table (see Appendix D). The life expectancy number listed next to that age is your Applicable Distribution Period.

Step 2:

Find the age the IRA creator would have been on Dec. 31 of the year the IRA creator died in the same table. Next to that age is the IRA creator's year of death Applicable Distribution Period. Subtract the number of calendar years since the IRA creator died from that number.

Step 3:

Your Applicable Distribution Period is the larger of:

- Your Applicable Distribution Period from Step 1, or
- The IRA creator's Applicable Distribution Period from Step 2[8]

Example:

Scott named his wife, Zelda, as beneficiary of his IRA. Scott died in 2014, the year containing his 86th birthday. During 2015, the year after Scott's death, Zelda will attain age 89.

Step 1 for 2015:

Zelda's Applicable Distribution Period for her own age (89) is 5.9.

Step 2 for 2015:

Scott's Applicable Distribution Period using the Single Life Table for the year 2014 is 7.1 years. For 2015, Scott's Applicable Distribution Period is 6.1 years (Scott's 2014 single life Applicable Distribution Period of 7.1 years, minus one year)

---

8 Regs. § 1.401(a)(9)-5, Q&A-5(a)(1).

Step 3 for 2015:

Zelda compares 6.1 years to 5.9, the Applicable Distribution Period for her own age. Zelda uses 6.1 years as her 2015 Applicable Distribution Period because 6.1 is greater than 5.9.

2016 & Beyond:

Here is a partial chart showing each year's Applicable Distribution Period from 2015 through 2019. The chart shows that, in Scott and Zelda's case, it isn't necessary to compare the two Applicable Distribution Periods after 2016 because Zelda's life expectancy will be the one that will be the Applicable Distribution Period for all years after that.

Year	Zelda's Applicable Distribution Period (Look up in Single Life Table Each Year)	Scott's 2014 Applicable Distribution Period from Single Life Table, Reduced by One for Each Year	Required Applicable Distribution Period (Greater of Zelda's or Scott's Applicable Distribution Period
2015	5.9	6.1	6.1
2016	5.5	5.1	5.5
2017	5.2	4.1	5.2
2018	4.9	3.1	4.9
2019	4.6	2.1	4.6

CHAPTER 15

Your Required Minimum Distributions: You're the IRA Creator's Surviving Spouse – Option 2, Make It Your Own IRA

Once you make it your own, you become the IRA's Creator

Required Minimum Distributions

AFTER YOU MAKE YOUR deceased spouse's IRA your own IRA, you're treated as though you are the IRA creator.[1] That can put off the day when Required Minimum Distributions begin until April 1 of the year after the year when you attain age 70½.[2] When you do take Required Minimum Distributions, your Applicable Distribution Period will come from the Uniform Table,[3] instead of the Single Life Table, thereby reducing your lifetime Required Minimum Distributions.

> EXAMPLE: Melinda died during 2014 at age 76 and left her IRA to her spouse, Nancy. Melinda didn't withdraw all of her 2014 Required Minimum Distribution before she died. Nancy must complete Melinda's 2014 Required Minimum Distribution withdrawal. After

1 Regs. § 1.408-8, Q&A-5(c).
2 Ibid, note 1.
3 Regs. § 1.401(a)(9)-5, Q&A-4.

doing so, and before the end of 2014, Nancy makes the IRA her own. Nancy's Required Beginning Date is April 1, 2017. Nancy's first Required Minimum Distribution will therefore not be due until Apr. 1, 2017.

EXAMPLE: In the above example, assume Nancy was the same age as Melinda. Nancy's first Required Minimum Distribution will be due by Dec. 31, 2015.

If you marry a person born more than ten yers after your year of birth, use the Joint and Survivor Table from IRS Publication 590.[1]

If the decedent's IRA was a Roth IRA and you make it your own, there will be no lifetime Required Minimum Distributions. And if you convert the decedent's traditional IRA to a Roth IRA, there also will be no lifetime distributions for you to take from the Roth IRA.[2]

---

1 Regs. § 1.401(a)(9)-9, Q&A-3.
2 Regs. §1.408A-6, Q&A-14(a).

CHAPTER 16

Your Required Minimum Distributions: You're Not the IRA Creator's Surviving Spouse

Your Required Minimum Distributions might be spread out over your life expectancy. But watch out for the five-year rule

THIS CHAPTER APPLIES TO you if you are the only IRA beneficiary and you're not the IRA Creator's surviving spouse.

Did the Decedent Withdraw the Year-of-Death Required Minimum Distribution?

By the end of the decedent's year of death, the decedent's Required Minimum Distribution must be withdrawn (see Chapter 9). If the decedent didn't do that, you must. If you must but you didn't, a 50 percent penalty tax applies.[1]

---

1 See Chapter 22. For an IRA creator, the Required Beginning Date is always April 1 of the calendar year following the calendar year in which that individual attains age 70 ½. Regs. § 1.408-8, Q&A-2. Where the IRA creator dies after April 1 of the year after age 70 ½ is attained without withdrawing the Required Minimum Distribution with respect to the year when age 70 ½ is attained, the IRA's death beneficiary must withdraw that distribution, but the decedent's estate and not the IRA's beneficiary will maintain responsibility for the 50 percent excise tax on the decedent's failure to withdraw it. Also, if the decedent's surviving spouse is the IRA's death beneficiary, that distribution should not be rolled over to an IRA

Five-Year Rule or Applicable Distribution Period?

Determine whether the five-year rule applies—check Chapter 8 to see if it does. If it doesn't, your Required Minimum Distributions must begin in the year after the decedent dies, over a number of years called an Applicable Distribution Period.[2]

Figuring Your Required Minimum Distributions Over an Applicable Distribution Period

Reminder: You must take Required Minimum Distributions from an Inherited Roth IRAs even though the Roth IRA creator didn't have to.[3]

Each year's Required Minimum Distribution is equal to the value of the IRA at the beginning of the year, divided by your "Applicable Distribution Period."[4] Your first Required Minimum Distribution must be withdrawn by the end of the year after the year when the IRA creator died.[5]

CASE 1: The IRA Creator Died Before Reaching the IRA Creator's Required Beginning Date

Find the age you will be on Dec. 31 of the year after the year when the IRA creator died in the Single Life Table (See Appendix D). The life expectancy number listed next to the age you will be on that Dec. 31 is your Applicable Distribution Period.[6]

The Applicable Distribution Period for the first Required Minimum Distribution Period (the year after the year when the IRA creator died) is the life expectancy you just determined from the Single Life Table. Each year after that, subtract one from the previous year's Applicable Distribution Period.[7]

---

of the surviving spouse. Doing so will incur the 6% excise tax on excess IRA contributions. IRC § 4973.

2 Regs. § 1.408-8, Q&A-1.

3 Regs. § 1.408A-6, Q&A-14. Also, the rules for making Required Minimum Distributions apply to an Inherited Roth IRA separately from individual retirement plans that are not Roth IRAs.

4 Regs. § 1.401(a)(9)-5, Q&A-1(a).

5 Regs. § 1.408-3, Q&A-3(a).

6 Regs § 1.408-5, Q&A-5(b) and (c)(1).

7 Regs § 1.408-5, Q&A-5(c)(1).

CASE 2: The IRA Creator Died On or After Reaching the IRA Creator's Required Beginning Date

Step 1:
Find the age you will be on Dec. 31 of the year after the year when the IRA creator died in the Single Life Table (See Appendix D). The life expectancy number listed next to the age you will be on that Dec. 31 is your Applicable Distribution Period.[8]

Step 2:
Find the age the IRA creator would have been on Dec. 31 of the IRA creator's year of death in the same table. Next to that age is the IRA creator's year-of-death Applicable Distribution Period. Because your first Required Minimum Distribution is for the year after the IRA creator died, subtract one (1) from the IRA creator's year-of-death Applicable Distribution Period.[9]

Step 3:
The Applicable Distribution Period is the larger of:

- Your Applicable Distribution Period from Step 1, or
- The IRA creator's Applicable Distribution Period from Step 2[10].

In other words, if you inherit an IRA from someone older than you, such as a parent, your own age will give you the larger Applicable Distribution Period. If you inherit an IRA from someone younger than you, the IRA creator's age will give you the larger Applicable Distribution Period.

The Applicable Distribution Period for the first Required Minimum Distribution (for the year after the year when the IRA creator died) is the Applicable Distribution Period you just determined. Each year after that, subtract 1 from the previous year's Applicable Distribution Period.[11]

> EXAMPLE: Hannah inherited her father Bob's IRA during 2007. Bob's IRA was worth $780,000 on Dec.

---

8 Regs. § 1.408-5, Q&A-5(a)(1)(i) and (c)(1).
9 Regs. § 1.408-5, Q&A-5(a)(1)(ii) and (c)(1).
10 Regs. § 1.408-5, Q&A-5(a)(1).
11 Regs § 1.408-5, Q&A-5(c)(1), last sentence.

31, 2007. By Dec. 31, 2008, Hannah will turn age 56. Her Applicable Distribution Period for her 2008 Required Minimum Distribution is 28.7. Hannah's Required Minimum Distribution for 2008 is $27,177.70. Her Applicable Distribution Period is reduced by one each year after 2008. Here are Hannah's Applicable Distribution Periods for the first five years:

Year	Applicable Distribution Period
2008	28.7
2009	27.7
2010	26.7
2011	25.7
2012	24.7

Hannah isn't required to take any Required Minimum Distribution for 2009 because there was a moratorium that year.[12]

EXAMPLE: Jeff inherited his younger sister Anny's IRA during 2011. Anny would have attained age 72 during 2011 had she lived to the end of that year. Anny withdrew her 2011 Required Minimum Distribution; therefore, Jeff won't have to. Jeff turned age 75 the year after Anny's death. Jeff's Applicable Distribution Period for the year after Anny's death is 13.4. Anny's 2011 single life table Applicable Distribution Period is 15.5. Anny's 2012 Applicable Distribution Period is 14.5. Jeff's 2012 Applicable Distribution Period for making his Required Minimum Distribution is 14.5 (Anny's year-of-death Applicable Distribution Period reduced by one).

---

12 Worker, Retiree, and Employer Recovery Act of 2008, P.L. 110-458, Section 201(a); IRS Notice 2009-82, 2009-41 I.R.B. 491.

CHAPTER 17

Your Required Minimum Distributions: You're Not the Only Beneficiary

Your Required Minimum Distributions might be spread out over the life expectancy of the Required Minimum Distribution Designated Beneficiary. But watch out for the five-year rule

Did the Decedent Withdraw the Year-of-Death Required Minimum Distribution?

BY THE END OF the decedent's year of death, the decedent's Required Minimum Distribution must be withdrawn (see Chapter 9). If the decedent didn't do that, you must. If you must but you didn't, a 50 percent penalty applies.[1]

---

1 See Chapter 22. For an IRA creator, the Required Beginning Date is always April 1 of the calendar year following the calendar year in which that individual attains age 70 ½. Regs. § 1.408-8, Q&A-2. Where the IRA creator dies after April 1 of the year after age 70 ½ is attained without withdrawing the Required Minimum Distribution with respect to the year when age 70 ½ is attained, the IRA's death beneficiary must withdraw that distribution, but the decedent's estate and not the IRA's beneficiary will maintain responsibility for the 50 percent excise tax on the decedent's failure to withdraw it. Also, if the decedent's surviving spouse is the IRA's death beneficiary, that distribution should not be rolled over to an IRA of the surviving spouse. Doing so will incur the 6% excise tax on excess IRA contributions. IRC § 4973.

Five-Year Rule or Applicable Distribution Period?

Determine whether the five-year rule applies–check Chapter 8 to see if it does. If it doesn't, your Required Minimum Distributions must begin in the year after the decedent dies, over a number of years called an Applicable Distribution Period.[2]

Who's the Designated Beneficiary?

Chapter 10 discusses who is the Designated Beneficiary.

Figuring Your Required Minimum Distributions Over an Applicable Distribution Period

Reminder: You must take Required Minimum Distributions from an Inherited Roth IRA even though the Roth IRA owner didn't have to.[3]

Each year's Required Minimum Distribution is equal to the value of the IRA at the beginning of the year, divided by the Applicable Distribution Period.[4] Your first Required Minimum Distribution must be withdrawn by the end of the year after the year when the IRA creator died.[5]

CASE 1: The IRA Creator Died Before Reaching the IRA Creator's Required Beginning Date
Find the age the Designated Beneficiary will be on Dec. 31 of the year after the year when the IRA creator died in the Single Life Table (See Appendix D). The life expectancy number listed next to the age the Designated Beneficiary will be on that Dec. 31 is the Applicable Distribution Period.[6]

The Applicable Distribution Period for the first Required Minimum Distribution Period (the year after the year when the IRA creator died) is the life expectancy just determined for the Designated Beneficairy from the Single Life Table. Each year after that, subtract one from the previous year's Applicable Distribution Period.[7]

---

2 Regs. § 1.408-8, Q&A-1.

3 Regs. § 1.408A-6, Q&A-14. Also, the rules for making Required Minimum Distributions apply to an Inherited Roth IRA separately from individual retirement plans that are not Roth IRAs.

4 Regs. § 1.401(a)(9)-5, Q&A-1(a).

5 Regs. § 1.408-3, Q&A-3(a).

6 Regs § 1.408-5, Q&A-5(b) and (c)(1).

7 Regs § 1.408-5, Q&A-5(c)(1).

CASE 2: The IRA Creator Died On or After Reaching the IRA Creator's Required Beginning Date

Step 1:

Find the age the Designated Beneficiary will be on Dec. 31 of the year after the year when the IRA creator died in the Single Life Table (See Appendix D). The life expectancy number listed next to the age the Designated Beneficiary will be on that Dec. 31 is the Designated Beneficiary's Applicable Distribution Period.[8] If there is no Designated Beneficiary, skip this step.

Step 2:

Find the age the IRA creator would have been on Dec. 31 of the IRA creator's year of death in the same table used for Step 1. Next to that age is the IRA creator's year-of-death Applicable Distribution Period. Because your first Required Minimum Distribution is for the year after the IRA creator died, subtract one (1) from the IRA creator's year-of-death Applicable Distribution Period.[9]

Step 3:

The Applicable Distribution Period is the larger of:

- The Designated Beneficiary's Applicable Distribution Period from Step 1 (unless you skipped this step because there's no Designated Beneficiary), or
- The IRA creator's Applicable Distribution Period from Step 2.[10]

The Applicable Distribution Period for the first Required Minimum Distribution Period (the year after the year when the IRA creator died) is the life expectancy just determined for the Designated Beneficairy from the Single Life Table. Each year after that, subtract one from the previous year's Applicable Distribution Period. [11]

You're in charge of figuring your Required Minimum Distribution if your share of the decedent's IRA is in your own Inherited IRA. If you're one of several beneficiaries of one Inherited IRA, you must figure out how much each year's Required Minimum

---

8 Regs. § 1.408-5, Q&A-5(a)(1)(i) and (c)(1).

9 Regs. § 1.408-5, Q&A-5(a)(1)(ii) and (c)(1).

10 Regs. § 1.408-5, Q&A-5(a)(1).

11 Regs § 1.408-5, Q&A-5(c)(1), last sentence.

Distribution is and be sure you receive that amount – otherwise you could have to pay the 50 percent penalty tax on any shortfall (see Chapter 22). You aren't ever responsible for the Required Minimum Distribution from any other beneficiary's Inherited IRA. That's because the 50 percent penalty tax applies to the person entitled to the IRA's payments.[12] After your part of an IRA is in your own Inherited IRA, you have no right to IRA payments from any other part of the IRA creator's account.

> EXAMPLE: Lee was named beneficiary of 50 percent of his father Clay's IRA during 2004. His older sister Madeline was the beneficiary of the other 50 percent. Lee's 50 percent was transferred, in a trustee-to-trustee transfer, to an Inherited IRA held for his benefit during 2004. Lee is therefore the Designated Beneficiary of his Inherited IRA. If Lee had not transferred his share to his own Inherited IRA by December 31, 2005, Lee's older sister Madeline would have been the Designated Beneficiary of Lee's Inherited IRA.
>
> As of Dec. 31, 2004, Lee's Inherited IRA was worth $850,000. By Dec. 31, 2005, he will turn age 45. Lee's Applicable Distribution Period for his 2005 Required Minimum Distribution is 38.8. His Required Minimum Distribution for 2005 is $21,907.22 (that is, $850,000 divided by 38.8). His Applicable Distribution Period is reduced by one each year after 2005.
>
> Here are Lee's Applicable Distribution Periods for the first five years:

---

12 IRC § 4974(a).

Year	Applicable Distribution Period
2005	38.8
2006	37.8
2007	36.8
2008	35.8
2009	34.8

Lee isn't required to take any Required Minimum Distribution for 2009 because there was a moratorium that year.[13]

---

13 Worker, Retiree, and Employer Recovery Act of 2008, P.L. 110-458, Section 201(a); IRS Notice 2009-82, 2009-41 I.R.B. 491.

CHAPTER 18

Your Required Minimum Distributions: There's No Designated Beneficiary

The five-year rule may apply, or you may be able to make Required Minimum Distributions based on the decedent's age

Did the Decedent Withdraw the Year-of-Death Required Minimum Distribution?

BY THE END OF the decedent's year of death, the decedent's Required Minimum Distribution must be withdrawn (see Chapter 9). If the decedent didn't do that, you must. If you must but you didn't, a 50 percent penalty applies (see Chapter 22).

Death Before Required Beginning Date

If the IRA creator died before reaching his or her Required Beginning Date and there's no Designated Beneficiary, the five-year rule applies. [1] The account must be emptied out by Dec. 31 of the year containing the fifth anniversary of the IRA creator's death. [2] A Roth IRA that has no Designated Beneficiary is always subject to this rule. [3]

---

1 Regs. §§ 1.401(a)(9)-3, Q&A-4 and 1.401(a)(9)-5, Q&A-5.
2 Regs. § 1.401(a)(9)-3, Q&A-2.
3 Reg. § 1.408A-6, Q&A-14

Death on or After Reaching Required Beginning Date

On the other hand, if the IRA creator died on or after reaching his or her Required Beginning Date and there's no Designated Beneficiary, the Applicable Divisor for the first year after the IRA creator's death is the life expectancy number in the Single Life Table next to the age the IRA creator attained (or would have attained had he or she lived to Dec. 31), minus one (see Appendix D). Each subsequent year, reduce the Applicable Divisor by one.[4]

Required Minimum Distributions from the Inherited IRA beginning with the year after the year when the IRA creator died are equal to the value of the account as of the beginning of the year, divided by the year's Applicable Divisor.[5]

> EXAMPLE: Louis died in 2010, the year when he attained age 75. Louis has died after his reaching his Required Beginning Date. But his IRA had no Designated Beneficiary. Louis's single life factor for 2010 is 13.4; the Applicable divisor for 2011's Required Minimum Distribution is therefore 12.4 (13.4 minus 1). Assuming Louis's IRA had a value of $525,000 on Dec. 31, 2010, the Required Minimum Distribution for 2011 is $42,338.71 ($525,000 divided by 12.4).

---

4 Ibid, Note 4.
5 Ibid, Note 4., Regs. § 1.408-5(b).

PART 4

REQUIRED MINIMUM DISTRIBUTIONS - YOU INHERITED AN INHERITED IRA

CHAPTER 19

Next in Line: You Inherited an Inherited IRA From Someone Other Than the IRA Creator's Surviving Spouse

You stand in the shoes of the first IRA inheritor when making Required Minimum Distributions

IF YOU INHERITED AN IRA from someone else who inherited it before you, and if that first IRA beneficiary wasn't the surviving spouse of the IRA creator, you must continue making Required Minimum Distributions in the same manner as the Designated Beneficiary of the Inherited IRA.[1] In other words, you just keep doing whatever the person who left you the IRA was doing. It doesn't matter if you're older, younger, or the same age as that person.

If you can't find out what he was doing, or if you want to make sure he was doing it correctly so that you will too, you'll have to figure out who the Designated Beneficiary was and how distributions were

---

1 Regs. § 1.401(a)(9)-4, Q&A-4. Under that regulation, a beneficiary who is living on the date of the IRA creator's death is still treated as living on September 30 of the year after the IRA creator's death for purposes of identifying the Designated Beneficiary. Thus, neither the identity of the Designated Beneficiary nor the life expectancies prescribed by Regs. § 1.401(a)(9)-5, Q&A-5 are dependent upon the continuing survival of the Designated Beneficiary. Because the Designated Beneficiary is finally determined as of September 30 of the year after the IRA creator's death, the death of the Designated Beneficiary can't change the identity of the Designated Beneficiary at any later time.

(or should have been) made to the person who left you the IRA. You can do that by looking for the first inheritor's situation discussed in the chapters in Parts 2 and 3 and applying the rules covered in those chapters to the first inheritor. Then, continue making Required Minimum Distributions to yourself in the same way.

Be careful about using the IRS' single life table for the previous IRA inheritor. The IRS can be expected to update the tables used for Required Minimum Distributions. When it does, let's hope the IRS says what continuing relevance the "old" tables might have (if any) for those who inherited an Inherited IRA .

Here's an example of how a second IRA inheritor makes Required Minimum Distributions.

> Charles inherited an IRA from his sister, Maria. The year after Maria died, Charles celebrated his 67th birthday. His Required Minimum Distribution for that year was the value of the IRA at the beginning of that year, divided by his applicable divisor of 19.4 (from the single life table). Each year, the applicable divisor is reduced by one. Charles died nine years later in 2012, at age 76, when his applicable divisor was 10.4 (19.4 minus 9). Charles didn't withdraw his Required Minimum Distribution in the year he died.

> Charles named his daughter, Paula, as his Inherited IRA's death beneficiary. Paula, as beneficiary of Charles' IRA, must withdraw the Required Minimum Distribution that Charles didn't withdraw in the year he died. After withdrawing that Required Minimum Distribution, Paula sets up an Inherited IRA and transfers her father's Inherited IRA to her own Inherited IRA in a direct transfer (Paula can't take an IRA distribution and make a rollover).

> Paula keeps using Charles' applicable divisor, reducing it by one each year, just as Charles would have done had he continued living. The year after Charles' death, the applicable divisor will be 9.4 (Charles' last applica-

ble divisor of 10.4, minus one), and so on. Assuming the Dec. 31, 2012 value of the IRA was $97,000, Paula's Required Mimimum Distribution for 2013 would be $10,319.15 ($97,000 divided by 9.4).

CHAPTER 20

Next in Line: You Inherited an Inherited IRA From the IRA Creator's Surviving Spouse

Make sure you know what you inherited and the circumstances surrounding it

IF YOU'RE THE SURVIVING spouse of a person who held an Inherited IRA of that person's deceased spouse, none of the IRA surviving spouse rules discussed in other chapters of this book apply to you. That's because the Inherited IRA was never an IRA of your deceased spouse.

First, Check to Be Sure It was an Inherited IRA

Look carefully at what you've inherited. A surviving spouse may elect to treat the IRA of her deceased spouse as her own, putting herself in the shoes of the IRA creator. If the surviving spouse did make that election, you've inherited the IRA from its "creator," and you didn't inherit an Inherited IRA. You should refer to Part 3—not this Part 4.

Here are the ways that a surviving spouse elects to treat Inherited IRA as her own (that is, an IRA of the surviving spouse):

- The IRA is either rolled over or transferred to an IRA held only in the name of the surviving spouse.[1] The title of the IRA will show the surviving spouse as the creator, rather than as the IRA's beneficiary (this is the most common); or,

- The surviving spouse failed to make Required Minimum Distributions as required of a beneficiary (requires tracing the Required Minimum Distribution history of the surviving spouse);[2] or,

- The surviving spouse made a contribution to the IRA (requires examining the IRA for contributions by the surviving spouse). [3]This method of electing to treat a deceased spouse's IRA as an IRA of the surviving spouse is rare because the financial institutions that offer IRAs generally won't permit a surviving spouse to make a contribution to an IRA of a deceased spouse.

Did the IRA Creator's Surviving Spouse Withdraw the Year-of-Death Required Minimum Distribution?

Make sure the Required Minimum Distribution of the decedent (in this case, the surviving spouse of the original IRA creator) is withdrawn before the end of the year when death occurred. The surviving spouse's method of determining Required Minimum Distributions is in Chapter 14.

The IRA Creator's Surviving Spouse Died Before Reaching the Surviving Spouse's Required Commencement Date

Chapter 14 describes the date when a surviving spouse's required minimum distributions must begin. That date is called the "Required Commencement Date."

If the IRA Creator's surviving spouse died before reaching the surviving spouse's Required Commencement Date, refer to Chapter 16, Your Required Minimum Distributions: You're Not the IRA Creator's

---

1 Regs. § 1.408-8, Q&A-5(b).

2 Regs. § 1.408-8, Q&A-5(b)(1).

3 Regs. § 1.408-8, Q&A-5(b)(3).

Surviving Spouse, but think of the Required Commencement Date as the Required Beginning Date. That means distributions may be made over your life expectancy, unless the five-year rule applies. For example, you must withdraw your first Required Minimum Distribution by December 31 of the year after the year when the surviving spouse died, or else you must withdraw the entire account by December 31 of the year containing the fifth anniversary of the surviving spouse's death.

The IRA Creator's Surviving Spouse Died On or After Reaching the Surviving Spouse's Required Commencement Date

Chapter 14 describes the date when a surviving spouse's Required Minimum Distributions must begin. That date is called the "Required Commencement Date."

If the IRA Creator's surviving spouse died on or after the surviving spouse's Required Commencement Date, refer to Chapter 19, Next in Line: You Inherited an Inherited IRA From Someone Other Than the IRA Creator's Surviving Spouse. That means distributions may be made over the remaining life expectancy of the IRA Creator's surviving spouse.

PART 5

GOING DEEPER

CHAPTER 21

The 10 Percent Tax on IRA Withdrawals Before Reaching Age 59½

Good news: The 10 percent tax on early withdrawals tax doesn't apply to Inherited IRAs

HERE'S A TYPICAL COMMENT I hear from IRA inheritors: "I heard I can't touch my Inherited IRA until after I reach age 59½." My answer: That's true for each of your *own* IRAs that you created, but not for any IRA you *inherit*.

If you make withdrawals from your own IRA before reaching age 59½, there's a 10 percent early withdrawal tax that's added to your income tax.[1] But the tax law provides several types of withdrawals that won't be penalized while under age 59½.[2] One type of withdrawal that won't be penalized while under age 59½ is a death beneficiary's Inherited IRA, no matter what age the beneficiary may be.[3] Unless you are the surviving spouse, you may skip over the rest of this chapter.

If you're the surviving spouse, you could wind up paying the early withdrawal tax anyway. That can happen if you roll over or transfer the Inherited IRA into your own IRA. That can also happen

---

1 IRC § 72(t).
2 IRC § 72(t)(2).
3 IRC § 72(t)(2)(A)(ii).

if you elect to make the Inherited IRA your own (see Chapter 15 for the ways to make that election).

What if you're the surviving spouse and you make part of the Inherited IRA your own IRA, but leave part of it in the Inherited IRA? The part you leave in the Inherited IRA will continue to be exempt from the early withdrawal tax. But the early withdrawal tax will apply to the part you make your own IRA. That means you can decide how much of the Inherited IRA you want available to meet your needs before you reach age 59½ and leave that amount in the Inherited IRA. The rest can be rolled over to your own IRA, which you're then less likely to touch because of that 10 percent penalty tax you'd have to pay on top of the income tax if you do make a withdrawal. The part left in the Inherited IRA can be rolled over to your own IRA any time. Doing so will mean starting Required Minimum Distributions when you reach your own Required Beginning Date, rather than by your Required Commencement Date. See Chapter 14.

Not all pre-age 59½ distributions will cost you a 10 percent early withdrawal tax. Here's a list of more penalty exceptions for IRAs (some of these, plus a few others, also apply to retirement plans set up by employers for their employees) – but beware: there are lots of definitions and special rules that aren't covered here. For more guidance on distributions that avoid the 10 percent tax, consult with your tax professional.

- Distributions made to the IRA creator attributable to disability (as defined in the law).[4]

- Distributions made to the IRA creator that are part of a series of payments that meet the IRS definition of "substantially equal period payments", based on either the life expectancy of the IRA creator or based on the joint and survivor life expectancy of the IRA creator and the IRA beneficiary.[5]

- Distributions made to the IRA creator because of an IRS levy on the IRA - which the IRS can do if its demand to collect

---

4 IRC § 72(t)(2)(A)(iii).
5 IRC § 72(t)(2)(A)(iii).

unpaid taxes goes unpaid.[6]

- Distributions to the IRA creator to pay qualified medical expenses (as defined in the law).[7]
- Distributions to the IRA creator, if unemployed, used to pay health insurance premiums.[8]
- Distributions to the IRA creator for higher education expenses of the IRA creator, spouse, children, or grandchildren.[9]
- Distributions of up to $10,000 (lifetime limit) for a first home purchase (if neither you nor your spouse hasn't owned a home for two years, you may qualify).[10]
- Distributions to certain individuals called to active military duty.[11]

---

6 IRC § 72(t)(2)(A)(vii).
7 IRC § 72(t)(2)(B).
8 IRC § 72(t)(2)(D).
9 IRC § 72(t)(2)(E).
10 IRC § 72(t)(2)(F).
11 IRC § 72(t)(2)(F).

CHAPTER 22
The 50 Percent Penalty Tax on Failing to Make a Required Minimum Distribution

The IRS may waive the 50 percent penalty tax

IN ANY TAX YEAR when the amount distributed from an IRA is less than the required minimum distribution, an excise tax must be paid on the shortfall at a rate of fifty percent.[1]

> EXAMPLE: Peter's 2014 Required Minimum Distribution was $36,000. Peter died during December of 2014. Peter's Required Minimum Distributions were being automatically withdrawn and paid into his personal checking account at the rate of $3,000 per month. Of Peter's $36,000 Required Minimum Distribution, $3,000 wasn't distributed because his monthly withdrawals were terminated upon his death. There's an excise tax of $1,500 due on the $3,000 shortfall.

The tax must be reported on Form 5329, Additional Taxes Attributable to IRAs, Other Qualified Retirement Plans, Annuities, Modified Endowment Contracts and MSAs.

---

1 IRC § 4974.

The tax law imposing the fifty percent excise tax on Required Minimum Distribution shortfalls authorizes waiver of the tax if the taxpayer establishes to the satisfaction of the IRS that (1) the shortfall during any taxable year was due to reasonable error, and (2) reasonable steps are being taken to remedy the shortfall.[2] Instructions to Form 5329 recognize and accommodate applications for waiver.

> EXAMPLE: Peter's daughter, Annette, was the sole beneficiary of Peter's IRA. Annette is the only person entitled to make a withdrawal from the IRA after Peter died. But Annette wasn't notified by Peter's IRA custodian that she was the beneficiary until February 2015. Thus, it wasn't possible for Peter's last $3,000 of his 2014 Required Minimum Distribution to be withdrawn on time.
>
> Because Annette was responsible for that last $3,000 withdrawal, the fifty percent excise tax falls on her and not on Peter's estate. Annette should make the withdrawal as soon as practical. Form 5329 should be filed by Annette with her 2014 Form 1040, U.S. Individual Income Tax Return. She should qualify for a waiver of the excise tax because her inability to meet the Required Minimum Distribution on time was beyond her control.

---

2 IRC § 4974(d).

CHAPTER 23

Don't Miss This Income Tax Deduction (if You Qualify)

Federal estate taxes paid on an IRA can be deducted on the IRA beneficiary's income tax return

IF FEDERAL ESTATE TAX was paid on the value of your Inherited IRA, and if taking withdrawals from your Inherited IRA means you'll have to report some taxable income, you may be able to claim an income tax deduction to offset some of that taxable income.[1] Even a small IRA can entitle you to the income tax deduction, as long as the total estate was large enough to cost some estate taxes.

These days, it takes a large estate to incur an estate tax. Generally, for decedents dying in 2014, the estate as of the date of death plus all lifetime taxable gifts would have to be greater than $5.34 million before an estate tax could be due. Going forward, that amount is indexed annually for inflation.

IRAs represent one of several kinds of income that an inheritor must pay income tax on when the decedent might have paid income taxes himself, but never did. This kind of income is known as "income in respect of a decedent" (IRD).

1 IRC § 691(c) authorizes an income tax deduction for federal estate taxes attributable to income in respect of a decedent includible in gross income under § 691(a). Taxable distributions from Individual Retirement Accounts constitute income in respect of a decedent. Rev. Rul. 92-47.

The amount of the deduction is equal to the difference between the amount of estate tax shown on the decedent's estate tax return (IRS Form 706), and the amount of estate tax that would have been shown on the decedent's estate tax return without including the IRA in the estate tax computation.[2] This can be a tricky exercise, because IRAs aren't the only items treated this way. Also, the computation of the estate tax as if the IRA wasn't part of the taxable estate might require adjusting a deduction in the estate tax computation, such as the marital deduction.

If there were several different items of IRD present in the estate tax return, each of those items will be paired with a part of the total income tax deduction amount.

The best way to find out if the deduction is available to you and the amount of the deduction is to ask the executor of the estate. In many cases, the executor is the only person who has all the information needed to do the job.

It may take more than a year to claim all of the income tax deduction. The amount of the deduction in any one year may not be greater than the amount of the taxable income for that same year.

The income tax deduction is listed on IRS Form 1040, Schedule A as an itemized deduction.[3] This deduction isn't one of the deductions that must be reduced by 2 percent of your AGI.[4] On the line next to the amount shown as a deduction, write in "Federal estate tax on income in respect of a decedent."

---

2 IRC § 691(c)(2).
3 Rev. Rul. 78-203, 1978-1 C.B. 199.
4 IRC § 67(b)(7).

CHAPTER 24

Don't Need Required Minimum Distributions? Some Ideas

Required Minimum Distributions that aren't needed can be saved and invested. Consider using those Required Minimum Distributions to beef up contributions to your own tax-advantaged retirement account

REQUIRED MINIMUM DISTRIBUTIONS ARE meant to empty out Inherited IRAs on a set schedule. But there's nothing stopping the beneficiary of an Inherited IRA from using those Required Minimum Distribution dollars to make contributions to the beneficiary's own IRA (which might be tax deductible) or Roth IRA, within the beneficiary's own annual limits for making IRA or Roth IRA contributions. Alternatively, if the beneficiary can divert part of a paycheck to an employer-sponsored savings plan, such as 401(k) account, it may be possible to increase the beneficiary's voluntary contributions by an amount, up to amount of the Inherited IRA's Required Minimum Distribution.

The income tax that applies to a taxable Required Minimum Distribution could be reduced or eliminated by making a tax-deductible contribution to a traditional IRA. The income tax is also avoided on the part of paycheck that's diverted to an employer-sponsored 401(k) account (or other qualified voluntary savings plan), because those diverted paycheck dollars directly reduce taxable wages.[1]

---

1 IRC § 401(k). Certain limitations apply to the amount that may be contributed without paying current income taxes.

An income tax "Saver's Credit" of up to $500 may also be available, in addition to any income tax deduction that may apply.[2]

If the amount you can contribute to your own retirement account is greater than the Inherited IRA's Required Minimum Distributions, you might be able to withdraw from your Inherited IRA whatever amount is needed to meet the maximum you may contribute to your own account.

Maximum IRA Contributions

Up to $5,500 may be contributed per year at the time of this book's publication. The maximum is adjusted based on increases in a government consumer price index from time to time.[3] Those who are at least 50 years old may contribute an additional $1,000, to reach a total annual contribution of $6,500.[4] But if taxable compensation for the year is less, only the amount of taxable compensation may be contributed.[5] Examples of earned income include wages, salaries, tips, and self-employment income. Check with your tax advisor to learn what rules may apply to you.

> EXAMPLE: Sisyphus owns and operates a boulder removal service (using a patented uphill transport process). During 2012, his net taxable income from services rendered was $4,500. Even though Sisyphus is now well over 50 years old, he may only contribute $4,500 to his traditional IRA.

Tax Deductions for Traditional IRA Contributions

Employed persons may be eligible to participate in an employer-sponsored retirement plan. If so, the income tax deduction for IRA contributions may be reduced or even eliminated.[6] The rule can also apply when an individual isn't eligible to participate in an employer-spon-

2 IRC § 25(B). This credit is not a credit that can cause the government to write a check to the taxpayer, and thus is not a so-called "refundable credit".

3 . IRC § 408(a)(1), incorporating by reference § 219(b)(1)(A); IRC § 219(b)(5). See further, IRS Publication 590A, Contributions to Individual Retirement Arrangements (IRAs), available on the web at www.irs.gov.

4 IRC § 219(b)(1)(A), (5)(A) and (C).

5 IRC § 219(b)(1)(B).

6 IRC § 219(g).

sored retirement plan, but that individual's spouse is eligible to participate in an employer-sponsored retirement plan.[7]

But that doesn't change the amount that may be contributed to a traditional IRA. It only changes how much of a contribution qualifies for an income tax deduction. Non-deductible contributions lower the taxable amount of future IRA distributions.

Contribution Limits for Roth IRAs

Roth IRA general contribution limits are the same as for traditional IRAs, but are also subject to income-based limits.[8] If the Roth IRA contribution limits apply, it may be possible to make non-deductible traditional IRA contributions. Later on, it may be possible to convert those non-deductible traditional IRA contributions to a Roth IRA. It's best to consult a tax professional before proceeding with such a plan.

---

7 Ibid, Note 6.

8 IRC § 408A(c)(2). However, contribution limits are integrated with traditional IRAs. IRC § 408A(c)(2)(B).

CHAPTER 25

Spousal IRA Rollover May be Possible, Even Though an Estate or a Trust is the IRA Beneficiary

A spousal rollover is likely available if the surviving spouse actually receives the proceeds of IRA distributions

WHEN A SURVIVING SPOUSE is named as an IRA's death beneficiary, the surviving spouse has the option of rolling over the decedent's IRA into the surviving spouse's own IRA – as discussed earlier, in Chapter 12.

In some situations, the surviving spouse may have that option, even if the surviving spouse wasn't named as the IRA's death beneficiary.

A spousal rollover is available if the surviving spouse has the right to actually receive – and does actually receive – IRA distribution proceeds, even though the IRA is payable to an estate or a trust. Whether the surviving spouse has that right requires understanding the surviving spouse's rights according to the terms of the will or trust (whichever applies). The best way to find out what those rights are is to ask the executor of the estate (if an estate is the IRA beneficiary) or the trustee of the trust (if a trust is the IRA beneficiary).

Here's an all-too-common example. Many IRA creators never get around to filling in their IRA beneficiary forms. When they don't, each IRA has default rules. In many (but not all) cases, the default beneficiary is the IRA creator's estate. If the decedent's will says the surviving spouse is entitled to the decedent's entire estate and the surviving spouse is the executor of the estate, an IRA rollover by the surviving spouse is possible.

Another example is when the IRA is community property. In the 10 states that treat marital property as community property, the surviving spouse's community property share of the deceased spouse's IRA can be rolled over, regardless of who's named in the IRA's beneficiary form. The states that have adopted community property laws are: Alaska (by election), Arizona, California, Idaho, Louisiana, Nevada, New Mexico, Texas, Washington, and Wisconsin.

Before making any distributions from the decedent's IRA, be sure to locate an IRA custodian who's willing to accept the rollover. Also, seek out the help of an attorney who can advise you about what your rights to IRA distributions are under the will or trust (whichever applies).

Because the IRS has not made it crystal clear whether a rollover may be made and what steps you should take to "do it right," it may be advisable to obtain a legal opinion letter. The purpose of such a letter is to say whether you are entitled to make the rollover and, if so, to detail each step you must take to accomplish it.

If you want the IRS to advise you in writing that you may proceed with the rollover, you may make a formal request by applying for your own private letter ruling. So far, the IRS has published over 100 PLRs allowing spousal rollovers when an estate or a trust was the beneficiary of an IRA or an employer-sponsored retirement plan. But in a few cases, the IRS has said "no." Submitting a PLR is costly: The IRS charges a substantial user fee and it will be necessary to hire a tax professional to help write it and submit it. But when the IRA's value is large, the cost can be worth the peace of mind.

CHAPTER 26

Disclaimers Can Reroute IRA Death Benefits

Just saying "no" to an Inherited IRA may be the right thing to do. But it isn't simple

SOMETIMES AN IRA BENEFICIARY will want to refuse part or all of the IRA. "Disclaimers" are used to do just that. It's a way of rewriting a decedent's estate plan.

Usually, when someone disclaims inherited property, that person is treated as though he died before the decedent did.

Reasons For Disclaimers

For example, David died survived by his wife, Lisa, and their two children, Connor and Camille. David named Lisa as a 50 percent beneficiary of his IRA and Connor as the other 50 percent beneficiary. After Camille was born, David never updated his IRA beneficiary form to include her. The IRA's beneficiary form said that if one of the two 50 percent beneficiaries wasn't alive when David died, that beneficiary's share of the IRA would pass to the other 50 percent beneficiary. Connor disclaimed his 50 percent share of the IRA. Since Connor is treated as dying before David, Connor's share became Lisa's property. Lisa made a spousal rollover of 100 percent of David's IRA to her own IRA and named both Connor and Camille as equal beneficiaries. Although this put off Connor's enjoyment of the IRA until his mother's death, this was a harmonious family and he was willing to do so to solve the inequity to Camille.

Another situation where a disclaimer might be attractive is when a relatively well-off sibling disclaims in favor of less well-off sibling. That disclaimer can help out the less well-off sibling. It will also lower income taxes payable on IRA distributions, when the less well-off sibling pays income taxes at lower tax rates than the well-off sibling.

Hire an Estate-Planning Attorney

To make a disclaimer, hire an estate-planning attorney. The IRA's beneficiary form must be analyzed to determine who will wind up owning the disclaimed IRA benefits. And, there are two sets of legal rules that must be watched: state disclaimer laws and federal gift tax disclaimer rules.

Who's Entitled to What's Been Disclaimed?

It's critical to know who will wind up benefitting from the disclaimer. This question means analyzing the IRA beneficiary document, the IRA custodian's documents that allow it to offer IRAs and state laws. If a trust or an estate was the IRA's beneficiary, disclaiming often becomes even more complex.

> EXAMPLE: Sophie, the daughter of a deceased IRA creator is named as 50 percent beneficiary. Alma Mater University is named as the other 50 percent beneficiary. Sophie might disclaim her interest, thinking that her share of the IRA will pass to her children because those children are listed as contingent beneficiaries on the IRA's beneficiary form. However, a close reading of that form may reveal that Alma Mater University will take what the Sophie disclaims, instead of her children.

If your disclaimer won't cause the intended person to wind up with what you wish to disclaim, it may still be possible to get the results you want by asking others to also make disclaimers.

The Role of State Laws
State laws are important because they govern property rights, such as the right to receive distributions from a decedent's IRA. Many states have specific laws that regulate disclaimers. If you overstep applicable state law, the disclaimer won't do its intended job.

Some professionals question which state's laws apply. There are three possibilities:

- The laws of the state where the IRA beneficiary lives,
- The laws of the state where the decedent lived, and
- The laws of the state that has jurisdiction over the IRA's contract.

Federal Gift Tax Disclaimer Rules
Federal tax laws impose a tax on significant gifts made by individuals. When disclaimers satisfy tax law requirements, it's possible to shift inherited property (such as an Inherited IRA) without making a taxable gift. Generally, the tax law defines a qualified disclaimer as a refusal to accept property (in our example, a decedent's IRA).[1] A qualified disclaimer must satisfy certain requirements:[2]

- The refusal must be in writing;
- The IRA custodian must receive the refusal within 9 months of the IRA creator's death (or within 9 months of when the individual making the refusal attains age 21);
- No IRA benefits have been accepted before the refusal is made;
- The person making the refusal can't direct who gets IRA benefits, and;
- As result of the refusal, the IRA passes either to the decedent's surviving spouse or to someone other than the person who made the refusal.

The IRS has said that a qualified disclaimer may be made after an IRA beneficiary has received a Required Minimum Distribution.[3]

---

1 IRC § 2518.
2 IRC § 2518(b).
3 Rev. Rul. 2005-36, 2005-26 IRB 1368.

Bottom Line: It's Complicated, Get Help

A lot can go wrong. It's best to hand the details over to a qualified professional.

CHAPTER 27

Unfinished Business: Rollover, Interrupted

It's possible to complete an IRA rollover that the decedent intended to make, but didn't, because of death

UNDER TYPICAL CIRCUMSTANCES, A distribution from an individual's own IRA (not an Inherited IRA) can be rolled over to another IRA, provided the rollover rules are satisfied.[1] One critical rollover rule is that the rollover must be completed within 60 days of the distribution.[2]

The IRS can waive the 60-day deadline,[3] and there are a variety of circumstances the IRS will consider, including:

- Errors committed by a financial institution, such as failing to follow instructions issued to complete a rollover;

- Inability to complete a rollover because of the IRA creator's death, disability, hospitalization, incarceration, restrictions imposed by a foreign country or postal error;

- How the IRA creator used the amount distributed (such as, in the case of payment by check, whether the check was cashed); and

---

1 IRC § 408(d)(3).
2 IRC § 408(d)(3)(A)(i).
3 IRC § 408(d)(3)(I).

- How much time has lapsed since the distribution occurred.[4]

For instance, if it can be shown that the IRA creator intended to make a rollover but that the 60-day time limit couldn't be met because the IRA creator died, the personal representative of the IRA creator's estate can ask the IRS to waive the 60-day deadline.

But getting the deadline lengthened isn't free. The personal representative has to apply for a waiver of the 60-day deadline by requesting a Private Letter Ruling. The IRS charges a non-refundable user fee for considering the request. If a professional is hired to write the request, submit it, and deal with the IRS on behalf of the individual making the request, substantial professional fees will be charged.

As of this writing, the IRS user fee is $10,000.[5]

Requests for Private Letter Rulings must meet IRS content requirements and must be sent to the IRS National Office. Although anyone can request a Private Letter Ruling, most taxpayers opt for hiring a professional who's experienced in making such requests.

If you really want to get a flavor for what's involved, you can look online at the requirements. Every year, the IRS publishes updated "revenue procedures" detailing the requirements and the user fees. Each year, many revenue procedures are issued on many more topics besides Private Letter Ruling requirements. They are numbered, beginning with the year. For example, Revenue Procedure 2016-1 is the first revenue procedure issued in 2016. Private Letter Rulings are covered in the first handful of revenue procedures issued each year. For 2016, 60-day rollover waivers are covered in Revenue Procedure 2016-4. The user fees are published in Revenue Procedure 2016-8. You may find the Revenue Procedures on the IRS website, www.irs.gov.

---

4 Rev. Proc. 2003-16, 2003-4 I.R.B. 359.
5 Rev. Proc. 2016-8, Sec. 6.01(4), 2016-1 I.R.B. 243

CHAPTER 28

More Unfinished Business: Switching IRA Contributions Between Different Kinds of IRAs After Death

A year-of-death contribution to a Roth IRA (including a Roth IRA conversion contribution) can be switched by the executor of the decedent's estate, after the decedent's death, to a Traditional IRA contribution and vice-versa. But look before you leap. And watch out for the deadline

THERE'S A WINDOW OF opportunity to reconsider the financial pros and cons of IRA contributions the deceased IRA creator made in the year of his death. During that window, contributions to a Roth IRA (including Roth IRA conversion contributions) can be switched to a traditional IRA. Likewise, contributions to a traditional IRA (other than rollover contributions) can be switched to a Roth IRA. Once a switch is made, that change will be treated as though the IRA creator decedent did it that way in the first place. IRA regulations call this switch a "recharacterization."[1] Once a switch is made, the switch is permanent: it cannot be reversed. [2]

---

1 IRC § 408A(d)(6).
2 Regs § 1.408A-5, Q&A-9.

The switch must be completed by April 15 of the year after the decedent died. That date is automatically extended to Oct. 15 if the decedent's income tax return is filed on time, or if there's a valid extension of time to file the return.[3]

But if you do consider making a switch, think long-term and make sure you take all the different aspects of that decision into account, such as tax rates that apply to the IRA creator; tax rates that apply to the IRA inheritor or inheritors (in some cases trust tax rates will apply); how soon the Inherited IRA will be drawn down, taking Required Minimum Distributions into account; expected investment returns; and, if Inherited IRA distributions will be invested, expected income taxes on investment returns.

> Example: Eddie converted his $300,000 traditional IRA into a Roth IRA the year he died, costing him $130,000 in federal and state income taxes. Eddie has died, and now his Roth IRA is worth only $275,000. It would be tempting to switch that Roth IRA back to a traditional IRA and recoup all $130,000 of income taxes. That could turn out to be short-sighted, because a decision based on today's investment volatility could turn out to look foolish over time, should the investments recover and grow significantly greater than Eddie's $300,000 conversion value. In addition, switching means paying income taxes on all future IRA distributions (Roth IRA distributions, on the other hand, are generally tax-free). It's a complex decision that requires a cool head and careful analysis. If the IRA is sizable, help from an experienced professional advisor is a good idea.

Deadline

An IRA switch must be completed by the due date of the decedent's income tax return. Generally, that due date is April 15 of the year after the decedent's death. More time is available. So long as the decedent's final income tax return is filed on time (including

---

3 Regs § 1.408A-5, Q&A-1(a)

an on-time filing when an extension of time to file has been obtained), the switch may be completed by Oct. 15 of the year after the decedent's death. And whenever the due date falls on a Saturday, Sunday, or legal holiday, the due date advances to the next weekday.[4]

The Executor Must Make the Switch

Only the executor or administrator of the decedent's estate or other person responsible for filing the decedent's final federal income tax return may make the switch.[5] If that person isn't the IRA beneficiary (or isn't the only IRA beneficiary), it's a good idea—and may even be necessary—for the IRA beneficiary to agree to the switch. If the executor makes a switch, the executor should file (or amend) the decedent's income tax returns consistent with the switch.

Types of Contributions That May Be Switched

A regular contribution may be switched.[6] For example, individuals at least 50 years old may make up to a $6,500 contribution to a traditional IRA. That contribution can be switched to a Roth IRA contribution, but only if the decedent's modified Adjusted Gross Income is below limits that change each year with cost of living adjustments. A death early in the year can be a game-changer, because AGI for that last year of life can be low compared to previous years, and the income tax rates might be low, as well.

Another kind of contribution that may be switched is a Roth IRA conversion.[7]

A switchable contribution that's transferred to another IRA of the same kind in a trustee-to-trustee transfer isn't a switch at all, but may still be switched after the transfer.[8]

---

4 IRC § 408A(d)(7).
5 Regs § 1.408A-5, Q&A-6(c)
6 Regs § 1.408A-5, Q&A-10, Example 2
7 Regs § 1.408A-5, Q&A-10, Example 1.
8 Regs § 1.408A-5, Q&A-7.

Types of Contributions That May Not Be Switched

- Tax-free rollover contributions may not be switched.[9]
- Contributions to a SEP-IRA or a SIMPLE IRA may not be recharacterized as Roth IRA contributions.[10]

---

9 Regs § 1.408A-5, Q&A-4.
10 Regs § 1.408A-5, Q&A-5.

GLOSSARY

Applicable Distribution Period – a number that is divided into an IRA's value as of the beginning of a calendar to arrive at that year's Required Minimum Distribution. The Applicable Distribution Period is based on IRS life expectancy tables. See Chapter 8.

Basis; Income tax basis – Generally, any amount that reduces taxable income. In the case of a traditional IRA, income tax basis means the amount that was contributed to the IRA, but for which no income tax deduction has been claimed.

Beneficiary or Beneficiaries – In the context of an IRA, a person, estate or trust entitled to receive IRA distributions after an IRA Creator's death. A beneficiary's rights are determined by examining the IRA's beneficiary form. If no beneficiary form is in force, the written documents establishing the IRA will indicate one more default beneficiaries. See also, Designated Beneficiary. See Chapter 10.

Designated Beneficiary – In the context of Required Minimum Distributions, the beneficiary whose age may be used to make Required Minimum Distributions from an Inherited IRA because that beneficiary meets certain tests. It is possible for an IRA to have one or more beneficiaries who are entitled to receive IRA distributions while, at the same time, to have no Designated Beneficiary because one of more of the tests to be recognized as a Designated Beneficiary aren't met. See Chapter 10.

Collectibles; Prohibited collectibles – Art, stamps, certain coins, and other property that may not be owned by an IRA. See Chapter 2.

Contribution; Regular Contribution; Rollover Contribution–Cash or other property transferred into an IRA.

Disclaim; Disclaimer–A written refusal to accept a gift given during a donor's lifetime or upon a decedent's death. See Chapter 26.

Distribution–Payment of an IRA's cash or property to an IRA Creator during lifetime, or to an IRA beneficiary after the IRA Creator's death. Generally the recipient of IRA distributions must report some or all amounts received as taxable income.

Five-year rule–Generally, if an IRA Creator dies before reaching his or her Required Beginning Date, the IRA must be completely distributed by December 31, of the year following the year of the IRA creator's death. (See also, Five-year rule exception, below.) See Chapter 8.

Five-year rule exception–Required Minimum Distributions may be made using the life expectancy method instead of under the five-year rule when an IRA Creator dies before reaching his or her Required Beginning Date, there is a Designated Beneficiary, and the Required Minimum Distributions over the life expectancy of that Designated Beneficiary are begun by December 31 of the year following the year when the IRA creator died. (See also, Five-year rule, life expectancy method). See Chapter 8.

Individual Retirement Account; Individual Retirement Annuity–Any of a family of retirement savings investments described in Chapter 2.

Inherited IRA–An IRA set up and maintained for the benefit of the beneficiary (or beneficiaries) of a deceased IRA creator and that receives the funds held in the IRA creator's IRA.

IRA–Abbreviation for Individual Retirement Account or Individual Retirement Annuity.

IRA creator–An individual who establishes and makes contributions to an IRA.

Life expectancy method–A method of making Required Minimum Distributions based on the age and life expectancy of a Designated Beneficiary.

Look-through trust or see-through trust–A trust named as beneficiary of an IRA that satisfies four tests described in Treasury Regulations. A look-through trust may calculate Required Minimum Distributions based on the age of a beneficiary of the trust. See also, Trust. See Chapter 10.

Prohibited transaction–A financial transaction that terminates an IRA and causes the entire IRA to be treated as having been distributed in a taxable distribution. See Chapter 2.

Recharacterize; Recharacterization–Switching a Roth IRA contribution (including a Roth IRA conversion) to a traditional IRA contribution, or vice-versa. See Chapter 28.

Required Beginning Date–The date when Required Minimum Distributions to an IRA creator must begin. See Chapter 8.

Required Minimum Distributions–Mandatory distributions from an IRA. An excise tax of fifty percent generally applies to any failure to make the distributions. See Chapter 8.

Required Commencement Date–The date when Required Minimum Distributions to an IRA Creator's surviving spouse must begin, when the IRA creator died before reaching the IRA creator's Required Beginning Date. See Chapter 14.

Rollover–An allowable contribution to an IRA of an amount equal to or less than the amount of a distribution from an IRA, provided the rollover contribution is completed within 60 days of the date when the distribution was made (other rules and restrictions apply). See also, Roth IRA Conversion. See Chapters 2 and 15.

Roth IRA–A type of IRA. Contributions to a Roth IRA are not deductible, and distributions from a Roth IRA are generally exempt from federal income taxes.

Roth IRA conversion—Rollover or direct transfer of any part or all of a taxable IRA to a Roth IRA, causing income taxes to be paid on the amount of the rollover or transfer. Only a surviving spouse may make a Roth IRA conversion of a deceased IRA creator's IRA.

Surviving spouse's election to treat IRA as own—Any action a surviving spouse of an IRA Creator takes resulting in the surviving spouse assuming the role of IRA Creator. See Chapter 15.

Trust—A legally binding arrangement whereby assets are held and managed by a trustee to benefit, in the manner stated in the trust, persons designated as trust beneficiaries.

Trust document, Trust instrument—A document establishing a trust.

Trustee—A person or entity who owns trust property in name only (in other words, a nominal owner; an owner in title only), and who administers and manages trust property for the benefit of trust beneficiaries in accordance with the terms of the trust document.

Trustee-to-trustee transfer—A transfer of IRA assets directly to another IRA, without making an intervening distribution to the person for whose benefit the IRA is held.

APPENDIX A
Stretchout Example – Traditional IRA

Facts and Assumptions

IRA owner	Catherine
Value of IRA at death	$300,000
Age of death beneficiary	65
RMD divisor - Single Life Table	21.0
Return on investment	
Before income taxes	6.0%
Effective tax rate	
Federal	20.0%
State (net of federal benefit)	5.0%
Net of income taxes	4.5%
Rate of income tax on annual RMD	
Federal and state	33%
Rate of income tax on lump sum distribution	45%

RESULTS

Amounts accumulated in investment account after Required Minimum Distributions end:

Cash out Inherited IRA upon death	$756,072.35	Amount A
Required Minimum Distributions	875,135.23	Amount B
Stretchout value (Amount B, minus Amount A)	$119,062.88	
Percent difference (stretchout value, divided by Amount A)	15.75%	

Present Value of Amounts Accumulated After Required Minimum Distributions End

The concept of present value gives us a way to translate the value of money that will be received in the future into the amount it's worth today, given an expected rate of investment growth. To understand present value it's easiest to start with an example of how investments grow. If $1,000 invested today will earn six percent, the investment's future value will be $1,060. Present value is the reverse of future value: if you'll receive $1,060 one year from today and if you expect your investments to earn six percent each year, the present value of that $1,060 is $1,000.

Cash out Inherited IRA upon death

$165,000.00 = Present Value of Amount A

Required Minimum Distributions

$232,652.59 = Present Value of Amount B

Stretchout value (Amount B, minus Amount A) $67,652.59

Percent difference   41.0%

COMPUTATIONS

Computation of Amount A

In this computation, the Inherited IRA is distributed in full upon death, causing the entire amount of the Inherited IRA to be taxed immediately.

The amount remaing after paying income taxes is invested over the same period of years that Required Minimum Distributions could have been taken. That period is used here so that the results of taking Required Minimum Distributions instead of cashing out the IRA may be compared.

Distribute IRA Immediately

Value of IRA at death	$300,000.00
Less: Income taxes on immediate withdrawal at 45%	135,000.00
Immediate withdrawal, net of income taxes	$165,000.00

Accumulation Account for Immediate Withdrawal

YEAR	Beginning Value	4.5% Investment Growth (Net of Income Taxes)	Ending Value
1	$165,000.00	$7,425.00	$172,425.00
2	172,425.00	7,759.13	180,184.13
3	180,184.13	8,108.29	188,292.42
4	188,292.42	8,473.16	196,765.58
5	196,765.58	8,854.45	205,620.03
6	205,620.03	9,252.90	214,872.93
7	214,872.93	9,669.28	224,542.21
8	224,542.21	10,104.40	234,646.61
9	234,646.61	10,559.10	245,205.71
10	245,205.71	11,034.26	256,239.97
11	256,239.97	11,530.80	267,770.77
12	267,770.77	12,049.68	279,820.45
13	279,820.45	12,591.92	292,412.37
14	292,412.37	13,158.56	305,570.93
15	305,570.93	13,750.69	319,321.62
16	319,321.62	14,369.47	333,691.09
17	333,691.09	15,016.10	348,707.19
18	348,707.19	15,691.82	364,399.01
19	364,399.01	16,397.96	380,796.97
20	380,796.97	17,135.86	397,932.83
21	397,932.83	17,906.98	**415,839.81**

= Amount A

Computation of Amount B

In this set of computations, only the Inherited IRA's Required Minimum Distributions are distributed over the number of years permitted. Each year, the Required Minimum Distribution amount remaining after income taxes are paid is added to the investment account.

Inherited IRA Performance and Required Minimum Distributions

Year	Beginning Value	RMD Divisor	RMD Amount	Value Invested for Year	6% Investment Growth	Ending Value
1	$300,000.00	21.0	$14,285.71	$285,714.29	$17,142.86	$302,857.15
2	302,857.15	20.0	15,142.86	287,714.29	17,262.86	304,977.15
3	304,977.15	19.0	16,051.43	288,925.72	17,335.54	306,261.26
4	306,261.26	18.0	17,014.51	289,246.75	17,354.81	306,601.56
5	306,601.56	17.0	18,035.39	288,566.17	17,313.97	305,880.14
6	305,880.14	16.0	19,117.51	286,762.63	17,205.76	303,968.39
7	303,968.39	15.0	20,264.56	283,703.83	17,022.23	300,726.06
8	300,726.06	14.0	21,480.43	279,245.63	16,754.74	296,000.37
9	296,000.37	13.0	22,769.26	273,231.11	16,393.87	289,624.98
10	289,624.98	12.0	24,135.42	265,489.56	15,929.37	281,418.93
11	281,418.93	11.0	25,583.54	255,835.39	15,350.12	271,185.51
12	271,185.51	10.0	27,118.55	244,066.96	14,644.02	258,710.98
13	258,710.98	9.0	28,745.66	229,965.32	13,797.92	243,763.24
14	243,763.24	8.0	30,470.41	213,292.83	12,797.57	226,090.40
15	226,090.40	7.0	32,298.63	193,791.77	11,627.51	205,419.28
16	205,419.28	6.0	34,236.55	171,182.73	10,270.96	181,453.69
17	181,453.69	5.0	36,290.74	145,162.95	8,709.78	153,872.73
18	153,872.73	4.0	38,468.18	115,404.55	6,924.27	122,328.82
19	122,328.82	3.0	40,776.27	81,552.55	4,893.15	86,445.70
20	86,445.70	2.0	43,222.85	43,222.85	2,593.37	45,816.22
21	45,816.22	1.0	45,816.22	0.00	0.00	0.00

Investment Account for Acccumlation of Required Minimum Distributions

YEAR	Beginning Value	RMD Amount	Less Income Taxes	Value invested for year	4.5% Investment Growth (Net of Income Taxes)	Ending Value
1	$0.00	$14,285.71	$4,714.28	$9,571.43	$430.71	$10,002.14
2	10,002.14	15,142.86	4,997.14	20,147.86	906.65	21,054.51
3	21,054.51	16,051.43	5,296.97	31,808.97	1,431.4	33,240.37
4	33,240.37	17,014.51	5,614.79	44,640.09	2,008.8	46,648.89
5	46,648.89	18,035.39	5,951.68	58,732.6	2,642.97	61,375.57
6	61,375.57	19,117.51	6,308.78	74,184.3	3,338.29	77,522.59
7	77,522.59	20,264.56	6,687.3	91,099.85	4,099.49	95,199.34
8	95,199.34	21,480.43	7,088.54	109,591.23	4,931.61	114,522.84
9	114,522.84	22,769.26	7,513.86	129,778.24	5,840.02	135,618.26
10	135,618.26	24,135.42	7,964.69	151,788.99	6,830.5	158,619.49
11	158,619.49	25,583.54	8,442.57	175,760.46	7,909.22	183,669.68
12	183,669.68	27,118.55	8,949.12	201,839.11	9,082.76	210,921.87
13	210,921.87	28,745.66	9,486.07	230,181.46	10,358.17	240,539.63
14	240,539.63	30,470.41	10,055.24	260,954.8	11,742.97	272,697.77
15	272,697.77	32,298.63	10,658.55	294,337.85	13,245.2	307,583.05
16	307,583.05	34,236.55	11,298.06	330,521.54	14,873.47	345,395.01
17	345,395.01	36,290.74	11,975.94	369,709.81	16,636.94	386,346.75
18	386,346.75	38,468.18	12,694.5	412,120.43	18,545.42	430,665.85
19	430,665.85	40,776.27	13,456.17	457,985.95	20,609.37	478,595.32
20	478,595.32	43,222.85	14,263.54	507,554.63	22,839.96	530,394.59
21	530,394.59	45,816.22	15,119.35	561,091.46	25,249.12	586,340.58

Amount B is the Ending Value (last column) after 21 years, $586,340.58.

Present Value of Required Minimum Distributions

YEAR	Required Minimum Distribution net of income taxes	Present Value ofRequired Minimum Distribution, net of income taxes
1	$9,571.43	$9,571.43
2	10,145.72	9,708.82
3	10,754.46	9,848.18
4	11,399.72	9,989.54
5	12,083.71	10,132.93
6	12,808.73	10,278.38
7	13,577.26	10,425.92
8	14,391.89	10,575.57
9	15,255.40	10,727.37
10	16,170.73	10,881.36
11	17,140.97	11,037.55
12	18,169.43	11,195.98
13	19,259.59	11,356.68
14	20,415.17	11,519.70
15	21,640.08	11,685.06
16	22,938.49	11,852.79
17	24,314.80	12,022.92
18	25,773.68	12,195.50
19	27,320.10	12,370.55
20	28,959.31	12,548.12
21	30,696.87	12,728.24
Total		$232,652.59

APPENDIX B
Stretchout Example—Roth IRA

Facts and Assumptions

IRA owner	Catherine
Value of IRA at death	$300,000
Age of death beneficiary	65
RMD divisor - Single Life Table	21.0
Return on investment	
Before income taxes	6.0%
Effective tax rate	
Federal	20.0%
State (net of federal benefit)	5.0%
Net of income taxes	4.5%
Rate of income tax on annual RMD	
Federal and state	0%
Rate of income tax on lump sum distribution	0%

RESULTS

Amounts accumulated in investment account after Required Minimum Distributions end:

Cash out Inherited IRA upon death	$756,072.35	Amount A
Required Minimum Distributions	875,135.23	Amount B
Stretchout value (Amount B, minus Amount A)	$119,062.88	
Percent difference (stretchout value, divided by Amount A)	15.75%	

Present Value of Amounts Accumulated After Required Minimum Distributions End

The concept of present value gives us a way to translate the value of money that will be received in the future into the amount it's worth today, given an expected rate of investment growth. To understand present value it's easiest to start with an example of how investments grow. If $1,000 invested today will earn six percent, the investment's future value will be $1,060. Present value is the reverse of future value: if you'll receive $1,060 one year from today and if you expect your investments to earn six percent each year, the present value of that $1,060 is $1,000.

Cash out Inherited IRA upon death

$300,000.00 = Present Value of Amount A

Required Minimum Distributions

$347,242.67 = Present Value of Amount B

Stretchout value (Amount B, minus Amount A) $47,242.67

Percent difference   15.7%

COMPUTATIONS

Computation of Amount A

In this computation, the Inherited IRA is distributed in full upon death, causing the entire amount of the Inherited IRA to be taxed immediately.

The amount remaing after paying income taxes is invested over the same period of years that Required Minimum Distributions could have been taken. That period is used here so that the results of taking Required Minimum Distributions instead of cashing out the IRA may be compared.

Distribute IRA Immediately

Value of IRA at death	$300,000.00
Less: Income taxes on immediate withdrawal at 45%	0.00
Immediate withdrawal, net of income taxes	$300,000.00

Accumulation Account for Immediate Withdrawal

YEAR	Beginning Value	4.5% Investment Growth (Net of Income Taxes)	Ending Value
1	$300,000.00	$13,500.00	$313,500.00
2	313,500.00	14,107.50	327,607.50
3	327,607.50	14,742.34	342,349.84
4	342,349.84	15,405.74	357,755.58
5	357,755.58	16,099.00	373,854.58
6	373,854.58	16,823.46	390,678.04
7	390,678.04	17,580.51	408,258.55
8	408,258.55	18,371.63	426,630.18
9	426,630.18	19,198.36	445,828.54
10	445,828.54	20,062.28	465,890.82
11	465,890.82	20,965.09	486,855.91
12	486,855.91	21,908.52	508,764.43
13	508,764.43	22,894.40	531,658.83
14	531,658.83	23,924.65	555,583.48
15	555,583.48	25,001.26	580,584.74
16	580,584.74	26,126.31	606,711.05
17	606,711.05	27,302.00	634,013.05
18	634,013.05	28,530.59	662,543.64
19	662,543.64	29,814.46	692,358.10
20	692,358.10	31,156.11	723,514.21
21	723,514.21	32,558.14	**756,072.35**

= Amount A

Computation of Amount B

In this set of computations, only the Inherited IRA's Required Minimum Distributions are distributed over the number of years permitted. Each year, the Required Minimum Distribution amount remaining after income taxes are paid is added to the investment account.

Inherited IRA Performance and Required Minimum Distributions

Year	Beginning Value	RMD Divisor	RMD Amount	Value Invested for Year	6% Investment Growth	Ending Value
1	$300,000.00	21.0	$14,285.71	$285,714.29	$17,142.86	$302,857.15
2	302,857.15	20.0	15,142.86	287,714.29	17,262.86	304,977.15
3	304,977.15	19.0	16,051.43	288,925.72	17,335.54	306,261.26
4	306,261.26	18.0	17,014.51	289,246.75	17,354.81	306,601.56
5	306,601.56	17.0	18,035.39	288,566.17	17,313.97	305,880.14
6	305,880.14	16.0	19,117.51	286,762.63	17,205.76	303,968.39
7	303,968.39	15.0	20,264.56	283,703.83	17,022.23	300,726.06
8	300,726.06	14.0	21,480.43	279,245.63	16,754.74	296,000.37
9	296,000.37	13.0	22,769.26	273,231.11	16,393.87	289,624.98
10	289,624.98	12.0	24,135.42	265,489.56	15,929.37	281,418.93
11	281,418.93	11.0	25,583.54	255,835.39	15,350.12	271,185.51
12	271,185.51	10.0	27,118.55	244,066.96	14,644.02	258,710.98
13	258,710.98	9.0	28,745.66	229,965.32	13,797.92	243,763.24
14	243,763.24	8.0	30,470.41	213,292.83	12,797.57	226,090.40
15	226,090.40	7.0	32,298.63	193,791.77	11,627.51	205,419.28
16	205,419.28	6.0	34,236.55	171,182.73	10,270.96	181,453.69
17	181,453.69	5.0	36,290.74	145,162.95	8,709.78	153,872.73
18	153,872.73	4.0	38,468.18	115,404.55	6,924.27	122,328.82
19	122,328.82	3.0	40,776.27	81,552.55	4,893.15	86,445.70
20	86,445.70	2.0	43,222.85	43,222.85	2,593.37	45,816.22
21	45,816.22	1.0	45,816.22	0.00	0.00	0.00

Investment Account for Acccumlation of Required Minimum Distributions

YEAR	Beginning Value	RMD Amount	Less Income Taxes	Value invested for year	4.5% Investment Growth (Net of Income Taxes)	Ending Value
1	$0.00	14,285.71	$0.00	$14,285.71	$642.86	14,928.57
2	14,928.57	15,142.86	0.00	30,071.43	1,353.21	31,424.64
3	31,424.64	16,051.43	0.00	47,476.07	2,136.42	49,612.49
4	49,612.49	17,014.51	0.00	66,627.00	2,998.22	69,625.22
5	69,625.22	18,035.39	0.00	87,660.61	3,944.73	91,605.347
6	91,605.34	19,117.51	0.00	110,722.85	4,982.53	115,705.38
7	115,705.38	20,264.56	0.00	135,969.94	6,118.65	142,088.59
8	142,088.59	21,480.43	0.00	163,569.02	7,360.61	170,929.63
9	170,929.63	22,769.26	0.00	193,698.89	8,716.45	202,415.34
10	202,415.34	24,135.42	0.00	226,550.76	10,194.78	236,745.54
11	236,745.54	25,583.54	0.00	262,329.08	11,804.81	274,133.89
12	274,133.89	27,118.55	0.00	301,252.44	13,556.36	314,808.80
13	314,808.80	28,745.66	0.00	343,554.46	15,459.95	359,014.41
14	359,014.41	30,470.41	0.00	389,484.82	17,526.82	407,011.64
15	407,011.64	32,298.63	0.00	439,310.27	19,768.96	459,079.23
16	459,079.23	34,236.55	0.00	493,315.78	22,199.21	515,514.99
17	515,514.99	36,290.74	0.00	551,805.73	24,831.26	576,636.99
18	576,636.99	38,468.18	0.00	615,105.17	27,679.73	642,784.90
19	642,784.90	40,776.27	0.00	683,561.17	30,760.25	714,321.42
20	714,321.42	43,222.85	0.00	757,544.27	34,089.49	791,633.76
21	791,633.76	45,816.22	0.00	837,449.98	37,685.25	875,135.23

Amount B is the Ending Value (last column) after 21 years, $875,135.23

Present Value of Required Minimum Distributions

YEAR	Required Minimum Distribution net of income taxes	Present Value of Required Minimum Distribution , net of income taxes
1	$14,285.71	$14,285.71
2	15,142,86	14,490.78
3	16,051.43	14,698.78
4	17,014.51	14,909.76
5	18,035.39	15,123.78
6	19,117.51	15,340.87
7	20,264.56	15,561.07
8	21,480.43	15,784.43
9	22,769.26	16,011.00
10	24,135.42	16,240.83
11	25,583.54	16,473.95
12	27,118.55	16,710.42
13	28,745.66	16,950.28
14	30,470.41	17,193.59
15	32,298.63	17,440.38
16	34,236.55	17,690.73
17	36,290.74	17,994.66
18	38,468.18	18,202.23
19	40,776.27	18,463.51
20	43,222.85	18,728.54
21	45,816.22	18,997.37
Total		$347,242.67

APPENDIX C
Uniform Life Table

For Use by:
• Unmarried Owners,
• Married Owners Whose Spouses Are Not More Than 10 Years Younger, and
• Married Owners Whose Spouses Are Not the Sole Beneficiaries of Their IRAs

Age	Life Expectancy
70	27.4
71	26.5
72	25.6
73	24.7
74	23.8
75	22.9
76	22
77	21.2
78	20.3
79	19.5
80	18.7
81	17.9
82	17.1
83	16.3
84	15.5
85	14.8
86	14.1
87	13.4
88	12.7
89	12
90	11.4
91	10.8
92	10.2

Age	Life Expectancy
93	9.6
94	9.1
95	8.6
96	8.1
97	7.6
98	7.1
99	6.7
100	6.3
101	5.9
102	5.5
103	5.2
104	4.9
105	4.5
106	4.2
107	3.9
108	3.7
109	3.4
110	3.1
111	2.9
112	2.6
113	2.4
114	2.1
115	1.9
116	0

Appendix D
Single Life Table
For Use by Beneficiaries

Age	Life Expectancy
0	82.4
1	81.6
2	80.6
3	79.7
4	78.7
5	77.7
6	76.7
7	75.8
8	74.8
9	73.8
10	72.8
11	71.8
12	70.8
13	69.9
14	68.9
15	67.9
16	66.9
17	66.0
18	65.0
19	64.0
20	63.0
21	62.1
22	61.1
23	60.1
24	59.1
25	58.2

Age	Life Expectancy
26	57.2
27	56.2
28	55.3
29	54.3
30	53.3
31	52.4
32	51.4
33	50.4
34	49.4
35	48.5
36	47.5
37	46.5
38	45.6
39	44.6
40	43.6
41	42.7
42	41.7
43	40.7
44	39.8
45	38.8
46	37.9
47	37.0
48	36.0
49	35.1
50	34.2
51	33.3
52	32.3
53	31.4
54	30.5
55	29.6
56	28.7
57	27.9
58	27.0

Age	Life Expectancy
59	26.1
60	25.2
61	24.4
62	23.5
63	22.7
64	21.8
65	21.0
66	20.2
67	19.4
68	18.6
69	17.8
70	17.0
71	16.3
72	15.5
73	14.8
74	14.1
75	13.4
76	12.7
77	12.1
78	11.4
79	10.8
80	10.2
81	9.7
82	9.1
83	8.6
84	8.1
85	7.6
86	7.1
87	6.7
88	6.3
89	5.9
90	5.5
91	5.2

Age	Life Expectancy
92	4.9
93	4.6
94	4.3
95	4.1
96	3.8
97	3.6
98	3.4
99	3.1
100	2.9
101	2.7
102	2.5
103	2.3
104	2.1
105	1.9
106	1.7
107	1.5
108	1.4
109	1.2
110	1.1
111	1.0

About The Author

MICHAEL J. JONES, CPA is a partner in Thompson Jones LLP, Monterey, California. His tax consulting practice focuses on estate planning and administration of retirement benefits, sophisticated wealth transfer strategy, trust and probate matters (both administration and controversy resolution), and family business transitions.

In addition to *Inheriting an IRA*, Mike is the author of *Final Regulations Governing Required Minimum Distributions*, a special supplement to The Pension Answer Book, Stephen J. Krass. He has written over 100 published articles. Mike serves as Chair of Trusts and Estates magazine's Retirement Benefits Committee. He has been quoted in New York Times, Forbes Magazine, The Wall Street Journal, Ed Slott's IRA Newsletter, Bloomberg Financial Report and others.

Mike has served as adjunct faculty at Santa Clara Law School, and has spoken extensively for the Jerry A. Kasner Symposium, Southern California Tax & Estate Planning Forum, Hawaii Tax Institute, American Institute of CPAs, New York University's Tax Institute, California CPA Education Foundation, and others.

Mike is an avid prone paddleboarder and surfer.

www.ingramcontent.com/pod-product-compliance
Lightning Source LLC
Chambersburg PA
CBHW050717280326
41926CB00088B/3080